A Tale of Two Streets

By Harry Gray.

The story of Wick Town Centre in the mid 19th Century

Published by

North of Scotland
NEWSPAPERS
Wick, Caithness, Scotland

A Catalogue Record for this book is available from The British Library.

ISBN 1 87170434 0

Published by North of Scotland Newspapers, 42 Union Street, Wick, Caithness, Scotland.

Introduction

Wick town centre has always been close to my heart. My own maternal Great Grandfather David Rosie was a journeyman tailor earning his living in Wick town centre.

For myself I began my working life as a message boy in the shop of James H Miller, Gents Outfitter, 104 High St. Wick, in 1950, working after school and all day Saturday. My first wage was five shillings (25p).

Forty eight years later I retired from a partnership in McAllan's of Wick and I am grateful to the very many people of Caithness and far beyond who made my working life such a pleasure.

I hope that the day is not too far distant when local shops are again to the fore, and our town centre once more alive, giving as ever, a caring and local service to the good people of Caithness and beyond.

Foreword / Preface

Some fifteen or more years ago during a conversation on local history, Trudi Mann said to me " You know, lots has been written on the herring fishing in the 19th. Century, but the shops and traders have been ignored, why don't you do something on that theme?" Well, that remark stayed tucked in the back of my mind, now finally, and long delayed, is my humble offering.

I am greatly indebted to a gentleman, signing himself "Wicker" who wrote to the Northern Ensign in the early twentieth century describing Wick in the middle decades of the nineteenth century. Without his keen eye and excellent memory, lots of information of people and events of 150 years ago would have been lost forever.

I am indebted to several people who helped me along the way, to Trudi, for the original idea, to Rachael and Gail of North Highland Archive for their patience, encouragement and generosity, not to mention coffee and bickies! To Sandy Gunn, a Weeker exiled in Thurso, for his generous sharing of all sorts of information, and to Andy Anderson for details on the history of Wick Baptist Church.

I would like to especially thank our daughter Amanda, who, although she lives down in Essex, has managed to convert my poor descriptions into the most excellent sketches and maps.

Most of all my grateful thanks to my wife Phyllis, for her patience and forbearance for the times I was "absent" either in North Highland Archive, buried in books, scribbling, prattling on, or attempting to type furiously on my P.C. She remains, as ever, my sounding board and anchor.

Over the period covered by this book, I have no doubt that businesses opened, flourished for a time, and closed, people came and went, all unrecorded. I very much doubt if I have been able to produce a definitive record of all the businesses in the two streets of Wick town centre. It therefore follows that all errors and omissions are entirely mine. I do hope that you will enjoy this dip into the streets of a Wick, long gone.

For Phyllis
Who like myself was once a counter louper.

The Illustrations

The Cover.   Drawn by Amanda Gray, from a map of the
                        Port and Vicinity of Wick, surveyed in 1839
                        and published 1857.

Characters   Robbie Scarlet, Tailor Lintie and Jamie
                        Harper Ross from John Horne's Caithness
                        Originals.

All other artwork and sketches: Amanda Gray.

Photographs and
Business advertisements   John O' Groat Journal and Northern Ensign.

Photographs,
Stafford Place and   By kind permission of The Wick Society
Louisburgh Street   from the Johnston Collection.

The Books.
J.T.Calder   Civil and Traditional History of Caithness
                          and Sutherland.

John Horne,   Ye Towne of Wick in Ye Oldene Tymes, and
                          Caithness Originals
Rev. T Brown D.D.   Annals of the Disruption.

Alexander Miller,
M.M., M.S.M.   Early Days of Freemasonry in Wick

Elizabeth Beaton   Caithness an Architectural Guide.

The minute books of Wick Town Council.

John O' Groat Journal and The Northern Ensign.

A Tale of Two Streets
Wick Town Centre c.1855

In the 1790's. Wick was a small hamlet with a population of approximately:1000. Pulteneytown was in the planning stages, but construction was more than a decade away.

Our town was built more or less following the line of our present day High Street - in those far off days known as Wick Public Road. The name, High Street, did not make its appearance until c.1813. The town ran roughly from the Parish Church (not the present building but two before this) down through the Camps area of the town.

Above the town, and on the slopes of what was then the "Hill O' Wick" an open common grazing space, a new village was being built on 33 acres of ground leased by Sir Benjamin Dunbar at 22/- (£1.10) per acre. Tenants would be expected to build on the leased ground a house to the value of £10.00. This new village was to be named Louisburgh, in compliment to Sir Benjamin's wife Louisa, and would remain an independent village until the extension of the Royal Burgh in 1883.

The main route into Wick from the south followed more or less the route of the modern A99, except that when the road passed Loch Hempriggs it swung to the west, and ran up over Newton Hill by the Dubh Lochs and down through the hamlet of Bankhead, where the railway station is today. It then continued over the brae and across the river by a wooden bridge, which was approximately 100yds upriver from the fountain area, and came into the town following the way of Kirk Lane and up into the main thoroughfare.

This bridge was rebuilt many times. A Wick Town Council minute of 1776 states that the "auld Brig" was insufficient and dangerous and that an advantageous opportunity may never occur again as there was timber lying on the shore off a vessel, lately wrecked at Sarclet. The council resolved to accomplish the project, estimated at £80, to build a bridge eight feet broad and fit to carry horses and carriages, the bridge to be supported by new stone pillars, and to cover the joists which are to go betwixt the pillars, with thick deals and planks. A mere two years later the bridge, which had been erected at so much expense, was in such great danger from horses and carriages passing over it that these were ordered to be driven over "the ford" unless the river be in spate. Failure to comply would suffer the penalty of a fine of 1/- (5p.) As late as 1800 the Town Council were still considering how best to proceed with a river crossing and at one stage considered pulling down the wooden bridge all together and using a cobble to ferry people and goods across the river.

Kirk Lane, once the main route into the town centre from the south.

Entrance to bridge street over the old bridge photographed around 1876

A painting of Wick in 1835 by Mr Munro of Wick. Notice the river width, and the lack of buildings on the west side of Bridge Street enabling a view of the Town Hall.

Eventually, and no doubt because of the impending development of Pulteneytown on the south side of the river, a new three arch stone bridge, with its distinctive hump and no footpath, was erected by the great Thomas Telford and opened in 1806. It would serve our town well until the present bridge was opened in 1877. How well Telford built is indicated in the following story.

In June of 1876 the Groat reported ; "On Tuesday morning the workmen engaged in taking down the old stone bridge, having removed as much of the centre as possible, proceeded to the mining. For this purpose, seventeen drill holes were made and charged with powder in the sides of the arches. On being fired at four o'clock in the morning, sixteen went off, and afterward the remaining charge shattering only the arch. After some hammering at the spring of the arch, the whole centre came down with a crash without doing any injury. We are glad to learn that Mr Johnston, the photographer, Wick, secured an excellent photograph on Monday, which is cabinet size, and will be valued as a curiosity from Wick."

The area we know today as Bridge Street, did not exist prior to the building of Telford's bridge. The bridge end, where the bridge meets the present roadway, was a small bluff or headland jutting out into the river with a sloping weed covered bank, where Riverside Residential Home stands today. The river then was much wider than it is now, a painting of c1835 shows small boats drawn up against the Kirk yard wall of the Parish Church. It is easy to see how this area eventually silted up to form our present day riverside.

Once the new 1806 bridge was opened and a new road driven through to meet the High Street, the development of our modern Bridge Street began. By 1828 our Town Hall and the Commercial Bank, now The Royal Bank of Scotland, had been built and the street, with a little imagination, was beginning to take on a modern aspect. The roadway was of compressed hardcore, dressed with shingle, and the pavement on the east, or Town Hall side, was eighteen to twenty-four inches above the roadway, whilst on the west side the pavement dropped by almost the same distance.

Bridge Street
Shops and people

So, who were the inhabitants and workers of Bridge Street in those far off days? Let's meet some of them.

We will begin on the corner of Bridge Street and West High Street, which today is cut away at an angle but then came forward to form a ninety degree corner.

We should bear in mind that almost all of this side of the street was rebuilt in the second half of the 19th. century, Riverside Home, Bridge Street Church and Clydesdale Bank all constructed between 1866 and 1875. Although the buildings have changed dramatically, we still have reference points to guide us along the street.

Back to the corner; the first shop here was run by Francis, or Francie Quoys, he termed it a draper's shop but in addition to his stock of cloth in single and double width with all the trimmings necessary for the making up of garments, he also sold tea and tobacco. He had a good reputation locally for his snuff and had a strong and loyal following who would use no other brand. He had his home in the Tibeth Vennel, set back and, with an iron gate set into the wall, it was reckoned to be one of the "swell" houses of the ancient burgh. The Tibeth Vennel is the old name for Tolbooth Lane which, in the 1840's, was known as Post Office Lane. The 1841 census has Francie and his wife and family living in this lane. Their sons John and David seem to have been twins, as in 1841 they were both aged 35. The same census shows an amazing ninety six people living and/or working in the lane. Francie was succeeded by his sons: John took charge of the shop and David oversaw the fish curing end of the business. Quoys harbour, or pierie, was in the river just beyond and opposite the present day Waterfront Nightclub. These piers were great places for local youngsters, fishing for sellags. John was very much a home bird and seldom ventured further than Bridge Street and the shore. One day he broke out of his normal routine. A friend of his had met with an accident, and was bed bound in Watten. John and a mutual friend made the arduous journey to visit the invalid and when they came in sight of Loch Watten John was struck with amazement and exclaimed,

"What an immense expanse of water, that'll surely hold its own with the great American lakes."

Neither of the brothers were adventurous enough to risk matrimony.

Next door to the Quoys was John Miller, also a draper, and famed locally for the quality of his needles. He lived over in Pulteney and every day at two o' clock he would lock up his shop and go home for his dinner. In later years when he gave up his shop, a Miss Sandison opened it as a fancy goods shop, selling wools, silks, crochet etc. Her father, deceased by this time, had had a shop on the opposite side of the road where he held stocks of various leathers and specialised in made to measure footwear of every kind, hand made on the premises. His business sideline was the sale of oil, a light grade, suitable for goose head or goose neck lamps, paraffin being unknown in his day. A Mr. MacAdie looked after the oil sales. He was known as a quiet, sedate man, meticulous in his dealings and never known to let the oil measure run over. At night a goose neck lamp with three "nebs" hung over the oil barrel to give light! What price health and safety? In between sales Mr. MacAdie filled up his day at the cobbling.

Now, back to continue our walk on the west side: next to John Miller was

ALEX. ROBERTSON, IRONMONGER, BRIDGE STREET, WICK, in gratefully acknowledging the support awarded him by the Public of WICK and COUNTY of CAITHNESS generally, for the last quarter of a century, has to intimate that he is still determined to supply his Customers with the BEST ARTICLES in the Trade.

A. R. refers with satisfaction to the numerous friends who have supported him during that lengthened period, and pledges himself that no effort will be wanting on his part to retain that patronage which has been so liberally awarded him.

———

A Large Quantity of Corn-Hooks, from the Best Makers.

Wick, August 31, 1853.

The year is 1853 and Alexander Robertson celebrates 25 years in business. What a range of tools and implements, how many can you pick out in the circle?
He also sold house furnishings and Gunpowder!!

13

a shop with what was regarded as the most splendid sign in town, A.Robertson, Ironmonger. This was a company with a long history of service to the town and farther afield, beginning in 1828 and carrying on well into the twentieth century, changing through the years from ironmongery to transportation, and introducing the first bus service between Wick and Helmsdale. In later times their garage was down at the end of Kirk Lane where a supermarket is today.

Stepping next door we find ourselves in the Farmers Inn, maybe for a wee refreshment from mine host Peter Kennedy. A later writer reminiscing on the old days, remarked that this was a very well run establishment and that he had never seen a drunk man come out of it. This business also had a very long term of service, continuing until Wick went "dry" in May of 1922. Later it was taken over by Fred Wares as a drapery store.

Adjoining the Farmers Inn was the shop of Alexander Bruce, another diverse business, draper and part grocer. Was this a strange mix? Or was Mr. Bruce far sighted and saw the advent of Tesco, Asda and the like, who are our modern equivalent drapers and grocers! Mr. Bruce was active in town affairs and became Provost in 1868.

Now we come to a rather strange property, which belonged to a Willie Alexander. This west side of Bridge Street sloped down to Kirk Lane and Willie's property had a sort of sunken storey on the slope, which, on street level, had two/three steps up to the shop front with a somewhat rickety wooden platform leading to the front door of the house. The tradesmen's entrance was by a door under the platform. John Sandison ran his drapery business here and John Mowat had a tailoring business upstairs. Drapery shops seem to dominate but we should remember that shops that sold Men's or Ladies' clothing or cloth or general household goods were all classed as Drapers. There were two houses in this property, one occupied by Willie Alexander and his family. Willie had a son, Dan, who had spent some time in the south and of whom he was extremely proud. He would say "Dan is an honest chap, never takes anything from the place he goes to, and always spends his money where he earns it".

The other house was occupied by an army pensioner, Lieut. Neil MacKay, who had lost an eye in action. He had retained his military bearing and was regarded locally as being "an ornament to Bridge Street." On fine summer afternoons the Lieut. would be seen, dressed in surtout and white trousers, marching to and fro between the bridge and the corner of High St. It was noticeable that, for some reason, on Friday afternoons and evenings his Malacca cane was planted on the pavement with greater emphasis. At this time, the local ex-service men were called out at regular intervals for drill and it was the lieutenant who drilled them, "in all his glory."

This brings us to Adam's Lane: this, today, passes between the Blythswood shop and the Clydesdale Bank and leads down to Kirk Lane.

We begin where the bank stands today. This property was of the same design as the previously mentioned Willie Alexander's building. The first business in this section was John Durrand, Druggist, who was helped in

An artists impression of Willie Alexander's property.

Lt. Neil Mackay, considered an ornament to Bridge Street.

NEW ARRIVALS!

JOHN SANDISON

BEGS respectfully to announce that he has got to hand a LARGE, CHOICE, and VARIED Assortment of

Spring and Summer Goods,

And those at Prices which are in strict accordance with his leading maxim—that of a Small Remunerating Profit, taking care to make QUALITY the primary consideration.

J. S. feels confident in inviting Inspection and comparison of the LADIES' DEPARTMENT, which is replete with every novelty for the season.

Silks.

PLAIN and FANCY, BLACK GLACIES, SATINETTS, OTTOMANS, & RADZMERES.

Stuffs.

BRADFORD LUSTRES, CIRCASSIAN CLOTHS, SPANISH and WELLINGTON CRAPES and COBURGS.

Robes and Dresses.

BALZARINE BAYADERE, OPHNE, BEN-GARA, CHENE BALZARINE, NORWICH, and BAREGE.

Woollens.

FRENCH MERINOS, DE LAINES, and PLAIN BAREGES.

Printed Goods.

MUSLINS, in JACCONET, ORGANDES, and BAREGE: CHINTZ PRINTS, and ROBED CAMBRICS.

Shawls.

LONGS and SQUARES, in every variety of Fabric.

Bonnets and Ribbons,

A BEAUTIFUL LOT, including the *Newest Styles.*

FLOWERS, FEATHERS, PARASOLS, FALLS, GLOVES, TIES, SEWED GOODS, and LACES.

BLANKETS, FLANNELS, BED CURTAINS, BED and TABLE LINEN, SHEETINGS, &c.

The GENTLEMEN'S DEPARTMENT comprises the following :—

WEST of ENGLAND and YORKSHIRE BROAD and NARROW CLOTHS, in all the prevailing colours.

TROUSERINGS and VESTINGS, in endless variety, embracing the most recent Fashions.

HATS, CAPS, HANDKERCHIEFS, AND TIES.

Country Merchants supplied on Liberal Terms.

Bridge Street, Wick,
April 12, 1853.

John Sandison's bewildering range of materials. Note the footnote, he also wholesaled goods to country shops.

JOHN CLEGHORN,

IRONMONGER, WICK,

BEGS respectfully to acquaint Families in Caithness, that he has been authorised to Sell

The Imperial Mangle, and Wringing Machine.

This Mangle has been designed with an express view to meet the great deficiency which has so long and generally been felt in this article of Household Furniture. It is very cheap, and is eminently adapted for the use of Private Families. The Imperial Mangle is of small dimensions, when packed, with stand, occupying only 32 inches by 12 inches.

J. C. is Agent for F. M'NEILL & Co.'s **Improved Patent Asphalted Felt for Roofing.**

Price ONE PENNY per Square Foot.

Orders received for every Variety of **Gutta Percha Goods,** such as Soles for Boots and Shoes, Tubes, Solution, Sou-Wester Hats, Pilot's Hats, Miner's Caps, Brackets, Pen Trays, Inkstands, Ink, Cups, Medallions, Vases, Fruit and Card Trays, Watch Stands, Drinking Cups, Flasks, Thread, Fire Buckets, Cricket, Bouncing, and Golf Balls, Galvanic Batteries, Bed-pans for Invalids, Chamber and Washing Bowls, Cash Bowls, Ornamental Flower Pots and Stands, Portmanteaus, Life Buoys, Fishing Net Floats, Life Boat Cells, Box Lids, Ear Trumpets, Stethoscopes, Speaking Trumpets, Soap Dishes, Electric Telegraph Wire, Balsam for Cuts, Sou-Westers, Syphons, Waterproof Canvas, Thin Sheet for Lining, Whips, Thongs, Ornamental Mouldings, Noiseless Curtain Rings, Communion Plates, Shaving Brush and Tooth Brush Trays, Lighter Stands. Finger Cups, Police Staves, Bottles, Carboys, Life Preservers, Paper Weights, Traces, &c., Manufactured by the GUTTA PERCHA COMPANY PATENTEES.

Gutta Percha Tubing is applicable for the following purposes:—

The Conveyance of Water, Oil, Acids, and other Chemicals, Liquid Manures, &c.	For Watering Gardens, Washing Windows, &c. For communicating between the Captain of a Ship and the Man at the Masthead, Helm, &c.
Drain and Soil Pipes. Suction Pipes for Fire Engines.	Ship Pumps.
Pump Barrels, and Feeding Pipes.	Ear Trumpets.
Syphons.	Speaking Tubes, in lieu of Bells, &c.
Ventilation &c., of Mines	

J. C. has on hand a large Assortment of Nails of every description and Shoe Tacks of all sizes, at very low prices.

Wick, July. 1850.

Gutta Percha was a hard rubber like material made from the extract of certain trees, native to Malaya. Note the range of uses for this material the shop by his brother Sandy. John lived in the house above the shop.

Next door was Mr. John Cleghorn, Seedsman and Ironmonger who, in his spare time, was an amateur geologist of no mean order and a great admirer of the eminent Hugh Miller, writer, naturalist and geologist, (1802-1856). The tragedy of Mr. Miller's suicide affected Mr. Cleghorn deeply and he held that if greater care had been taken the calamity might have been averted. When the British Fisheries Society was negotiating the building of the new harbour, Mr.Cleghorn was dead set against the idea, advocating improving the river and building the harbour on the north side of the bay. He also served on Wick Town Council as councillor and magistrate.

Mr. Cleghorn's neighbour was Mr. Robert Leith, Druggist. It appears that this property was known as Raeburn's tenement, a tenement then being a piece of ground on which a property was built and not in the modern sense of the word. An entry in Wick Town Council minutes for January 3rd. 1841 states that the property known as Raeburn's Tenement, presently occupied by Mrs. Mackay, was to be relinquished by her on Whitsunday and was to be re-let to Mr Robert Leith of Wick for the sum of £15.00 per annum, the offer being received from William Leith, Druggist, Wick, Alexander Sutherland, Merchant, Swiney, and David Wares, Merchant, Wick on behalf of Robert Leith.

Above Leith's shop was Donald Bremner, Tailor, who lived in and worked from the same premises, which had access by a wooden platform to the side. Many buildings then did not have internal staircases, the upper floors being accessed by external steps. Below Leith's shop in a sort of basement lived John and Euphemia Harper. It was said that they carried on a sort of nondescript business for some years. John was a dyer to trade, but was also " a great many other things!" maybe a bit of a wheeler dealer. One day John simply vanished, did not leave a forwarding address and was never heard of again, at least not by Euphemia!

A Barber's Tale

Now we meet King Otho, a great character in the ancient burgh and in the modern town of Pulteney, wig maker and barber extraordinaire. His origins were in Inverness-shire and he may have done a bit of travelling, possibly as a "gentleman's gentleman." His proud boast was that he had once shaved King Otho of Greece, that would be enough for Weekers to give him his soubriquet. His real name, according to Wicker's column in the Northern Ensign, was John Fraser although John Horne has his name as Hepburn, yet he appears in Slater's Business Directory of 1852 as John Fraser; whichever it was we will call him King Otho. He kept two shops, one, his winter shop, in Bridge Street, and the other, his summer shop, was in the Shore Road because of the huge influx of fisher folk, almost guaranteeing him good trade. This Shore Road establishment was termed, "The Wigwam." This roadway, in the mid 19th century was not the Shore Road of today and King Otho's premises was about halfway up, and built into a niche cut out of the boulder clay, and into this square his "Wigwam" was fitted. The doorway was reached by a short set of steps; to the left was his barbers shop and on the right was his inner sanctum; the whole being roofed in canvas. A legend on the shutter proclaimed that the worthy barber made and repaired wigs and frontlets, and also compounded his own macassar (an oil used by both sexes as a hair dressing). Mr Fraser lodged with an elderly couple in Lower Pulteney where he lived and died. Mostly he was frugal and abstemious, but now and then he went on a "turrymurry" or a "bender" which would last for a week or so. His benders usually happened in the quiet season after the fishing, and he closed up shop for the duration; but at times bender and work overlapped, as the following wee tale reveals.

Now and again John took a little more of the barley bree than was good for him and a story is told of a certain young man, we'll call him Sandy, who went into King Otho's Shore Road establishment for a shave whilst his pals lounged against the wall opposite. After only a few minutes Sandy burst out of the door, panic stricken, his face covered in shaving soap, causing much merriment to his cronies. After he had cleared his face of soap suds, he explained that as the barber was lathering his face, he could see from his antics that he was drunk, and he wondered, that if he was this bad with the soap brush, what would happen when the razor came into play so he waited until Otho turned his back to strop the razor and bolted, unshaven, but unharmed. On his death Mr. J.G.Duncan wrote a poem in memory of the genial and gentle King Otho and his long demolished Wigwam.

On the death of John Fraser.

Alas poor Fraser too soon thy razor, hath dropped with thee into the tomb,
And now an unshaven silent gazer, I pass thy wigwam, wrapped in gloom,
No smoke in graceful curve ascends from out its chimney stalk so humble,
Its canvas roof in frailty bends, and down the Shore Road soon will tumble.
No dapper wig, no fronted nobby now glimmer through its window panes,

For dust and death surmount the hobby, and we must walk with hairless brains,

Though closed the door and fast the shutter, yet still I feel the wonted craving,

To enter in without a flutter, for chaff and comfortable shaving,

But sign of life, there's none around, save one bald, sickly, solemn scorrie,

Which from the roof screams out a sound, like "Otho, I am truly sorry,"

Thus o'er the palaces of kings, and huts, and halls be writ, shall one day,

That truth, which little comfort brings, "Sic transit gloria mundi"

Fraser, no more thy curious smile shall move each old familiar passer,

To patronise your favourite oil, that virtuous compound, called macassar,

Again, no urchin fresh from school, shall hear you ask with air so grave, sir

What strikes him as uncommon cool, the startling question, "poll or shave sir?"

Your water's cold, your soap is mould, some chins are spacious fields of stubble,

Why should your virtues be untold, who s(h)aved us such a world of trouble.

Even up to the middle decades of the 20th century folk used linen covers on the backs of armchairs and settees, these were sold as anti-macassars as they prevented the Macassar oil from staining the chair back.

Leaving King Otho's winter shop in Bridge Street we move next door into the premises of another John Sandison, also a draper. He had moved from a small shop into this more commodious premises in May of 1851 and was "fair taken" by how well his goods looked in the larger shop.

We are now at the top of Miller Lane which leads down to Kirk Lane and the supermarket area. In olden times this lane still led down to Kirk Lane but with a dramatically different appearance. On the first corner stood Mrs MacKay's public house while Steven's painters business was on the opposite corner. Across the way were the business premises of Alex Tait's Smiddy and Alex Malcolm's coach building business. In modern terms we are where the small car park and the rear entrance to Houston's is. On the roadway Alex Tait would put iron rims onto cartwheels. What excitement for youngsters to watch as four or five men with long pincers picked up the red hot rim from the blazing circular fire and placed it round the wheel, then the hammering, the water being poured, steam and smoke billowing ----- a red letter day indeed!

At the top of Miller Lane, where the Bank of Scotland is today, there was a set of steps, leading to a lane which ran diagonally down the brae and led to the river. At the foot of these steps on the right hand side, Gideon Johnstone had his house and his baking oven; more about Gideon later. On the left side, and a little further down, was Sandy Bremners joiner shop. Opposite him was the joinery premises of Donald Dunbar. This gentleman was the woodwork contractor for the Parish Church that opened in 1830. This must have been quite a contract; the roof beams alone are sixty-six feet long, ten inches wide and fifteen inches deep, in Russian red pine, selected and brought to Wick by Captain Munro in his ship "Bittern." The beams were towed upriver to the side of the Kirk Yard, which indicates the width of our river in those far off days. When the tide was fully in and the beams afloat, local youngsters had a wonderful time leaping from beam to beam, playing chase or dare over the slippery wood and probably hoping someone would fall into the river and add more fun to the game; boy, what fun! Mr Dunbar must have had great skills to manoeuvre the great beams from the river, all the way up to the wall heads of the Kirk, where they remain to this day still holding one of the largest unsupported Kirk roofs in Scotland. It was remarked by the building inspector of the day that Mr Dunbar had less wood left over after the Kirk contract than another joiner, James Mackay, had after the town jail. Another remarked that he only had enough wood left over to make a footstool; if this was the case, then, good estimating! Mr. Dunbar also had a hand in the building and/or reworking of the Wick Episcopal Church Wick Bridge Street Church, and the Kirks at Strathy, Keiss and Watten as well as Thurso Castle, Barrogill Castle (now Castle of Mey) and Dunbeath Castle. The place where he cured his wood can still be seen in Victoria Place, in the small entry beside Shearer's D.I.Y the slits in the wall are clearly visible.

Between Mr Dunbar's shop and the river stood the dye works, operated by Mr Noble and his son. Beside the works there was an opening in the river wall, with a short pier jutting out into the river. At the point of this pier, and to the lower side, was a deep hole, possibly dredged, where, after the dyeing process, the articles were rinsed out and worked with a long wooden pole. After this rinsing the river water would turn a very strange colour but it did not seem to affect the "flukies" (flat fish) which local children still caught in the hole. Organic dye perhaps? When Mr Noble passed away his son continued with the business but the later reconstruction of this part of town caused him to move premises. The ordnance survey map of 1872 shows the dye works in Victoria Place, beside the river and a little way up from where the Salvation Army have their Church today.

Now, back to the top of Miller Lane where the Bank of Scotland stands today. The property here consisted of two shops and a house. The house was occupied by James Sutherland, auctioneer, and the first shop by James Sinclair, a boot and shoe merchant. After James Sutherland the house was taken by Dr Smellie. Wicker, our contributor to the "Ensign", remembers Dr Smellie as a very nice man, remarking that a visit from the good doctor was a curative, almost a cure without medicine. However, Wicker took exception when Dr Smellie advised Wicker's mother to apply a mustard poultice to his chest for twenty minutes, the longest twenty minutes of Wicker's life. The next day he complained to Dr Smellie about the treatment and the good doctor simply laughed.

Next door is the last property on this side of Bridge Street and was occupied by Mr Campbell, a barber, who was, in his spare time, a bird fancier. This property was in extremely poor condition.

From the end of Campbell's shop to the bridge end ran a dyke about four feet high and then from the bridge end a steep set of steps went down to the end of the Kirk Lane area. This stairway is still there today, although reconstructed. The whole area from Campbell's shop to the river was waste ground, covered in weeds and nettles, but a productive source of worms for the fishing fraternity. It is on this piece of ground that the Bridge Street Church and the Riverside Home stand today.

Bridge Street East

We now move across the road and meet some of the people who lived and worked on the east side of Bridge Street.

The first building next to the Bridge end is of course The Royal Bank of Scotland, originally the Commercial Bank, an elegant, modern looking building, adding much to the appearance of the street. It is in fact one of the oldest buildings in the street, opening in 1830, and at the time referred to as Rhind's bank. Josiah Rhind was the manager, with James Mackay as his second in command. Mr Rhind was Provost of our town in 1838 and again in 1843, a very prominent and well respected citizen. His son, Henry Rhind, bequeathed £7000.00 to fund a training school in domestic servant skills for orphan girls. A house which had been built in East Banks by Mr George Cormack, cooper, was acquired and extended for the purpose, and became known as Rhind House.

Victoria Place comes next and was then much narrower than it is today and led down into a large open space, extending from the north jail yard wall to the riverbank, known as The Muckle Yard. In 1841 the Council decided to advertise the yard for rent at £3 per annum and if this failed to be so let, the Council would consider converting the yard into a weekly market for cattle. In February of 1842 part of the yard was let to Donald

Bremner for the purpose of boat building with the proviso that if he was not busy at the boat building, he would allow townsfolk space to bleach their clothes in the area. In 1844 the Council decided to widen Victoria Place, improve the roadway and create a proper road link between Bridge St. and the Camps area. This effectively cut the Muckle Yard into two parts. The part immediately behind the Town Hall was feued out to Caithness Prison Board and the ground on the river side was divided up into lots and sold off. Things moved slowly (so what's new?) and the Council made an alteration to the plan in 1848 mentioning the road "by the Chapel now building." This would be the Evangelical Union Church, which is today the Salvation Army Church.

All this was behind our Town Hall, the building of which began in 1825 and opened in 1828. Originally it was called The Town and County Buildings, which contained the tolbooth, or jail, in the wings, and also the Sheriff Court, the latter being no more than a small chamber, half of which was taken up by the bench and lawyers seat, so that there was no public space. At this time the Sheriff, or Beeg Shirra as he was known, was Sheriff Thompson with Sheriff Grieg as substitute. The other functionaries were Procurator Fiscal – John Henderson, Town Clerk – William Miller, Sheriff Clerk – Robert MacLachlan, Depute – James Craig, Messenger at Arms – George Bremner, Jailor – Henry Osbourne, Town Officer – Alexander Phimister. The latter had many responsibilities including the Town Garden where, it was said, the Bourtree (elder) grew abundantly. He was also appointed lamplighter when the new fangled gas street lighting was piped into the town centre in 1843.

In September of that year Provost Bruce was reporting that the new lamp posts had been erected and fitted up (by John Brims and Donald Bruce) and the grand switch on or rather, light up, was fixed for October 4th. 1843. The cost of the Burgh lamp posts had been met by the generous support of the Duke of Sutherland who had donated £15 towards the installation. A plaque was placed on the eastern parapet of the bridge under one of the lamp posts. It read; "Erected at the expense of His Grace The Duke of Sutherland, Superior of this Burgh, who visited on 6th September 1843." The "Groat" rushed into print, tongue firmly in cheek, suggesting that locals felt that future generations would take the plaque to mean that His Grace had paid for the bridge rather than the lamp posts --- very misleading! (Did this plaque survive the demolition of the "Auld Brig?" Is it still around?) The great day dawned, or rather set, and Wick was duly illuminated. The excitement merited two column inches in the Groat of 6th October 1843 which rather laconically reported;- "On Wednesday evening last, being the day of the solemnization of the nuptials of Lady Evelyn Gower and Lord Blantyre, the street lamps of Wick, erected at the expense of His Grace The Duke of Sutherland were lit for the first time. Although a vast accommodation for the town, many more lamp posts are required to throw sufficient light on the streets. At any rate, those at present erected should have more powerful burners, for the present are very dim. The "batwing" or "fishtail" are the most suitable ---- but we must not grumble."

Of course Wickers had become accustomed to the gas light. As far back as 1838 Mr Henderson, Distiller of Pulteneytown, had installed a private gas works in his Huddart Street premises. This gentleman was chairman of the Wick and Pulteneytown Gas Light Company which had been formed in 1839. Many of the shops and businesses had installed gas lighting in March of 1841. The light was really just a flickering flame, for this was long before the incandescent gas mantle.

Our town jail was visited by the Inspector of Prisons and a report of his findings was received by the Council in November 1842. The inspector found that the improvements he had called for last year were in the late planning stage, then as now the council were good at making haste, slowly. The average number of prisoners was four. Contracts had not been acted on but the supplies were small there being few prisoners. A few omissions in the registers were noted. As to work, the prisoners had hitherto not been allotted tasks. The prisoners were taught reading and writing by the keeper and matron (Henry Osbourne and his good lady) and were tested once a month by the Chaplain and the results noted. Reverend David Mitchell visited twice a week for spiritual consolation. He was minister of what is now Pulteney Parish Church and his remuneration for this service was £20 per year. The surgeon reported "that the general health of the prisoners is good although some suffer from damp in the winter, but work in hand will correct the situation. The keeper states that the behaviour of the prisoners is generally good, the general state of the prison is creditable to Mr Osbourne." The inspector recommended the adoption of the new dietary system and that clothing for females should be warmer. (Prisoners' rights alive and well in Wick in 1842!) This Henry Osbourne had a son, also Henry, who was an avid naturalist and friend of Robert Innes Shearer whose work on Birds and Mammals of Caithness is covered in detail in the book by Hugh Clark and Robin M. Sellars published in early 2005.

While we are on the subject of the Town Council, they were at this time greatly concerned about the state of the streets and general sanitation. This was long before running water and sanitation as we today would know it. Most houses had a midden into which all the household dirt and filth was thrown; these middens were known as the "fulzie." The collection of this waste was put up for roup (auction) each year, at the upset price of £5, and this contract was held for years by James Henderson (Distiller of Pulteneytown) who employed a man to collect it in a horse drawn cart. This man would ring a bell to let people know that he was on his rounds. In a Town Council minute of 1846 Mr Henderson is referred to with the grandiose title, Tacksman of the Fulzie. This means of waste collection and disposal was traditional. Away back in the 1770/80s Baillie Macleay farmed at Thrumster and used the fulzie as manure for his crops. It was said that his crops were excellent, showing the great efficacy of The Royal Burgh's dirt. As a side note this gentleman, later Provost, had an inn in Wick with a reputation for good service, clean beds, fresh food and an excellent claret for half a crown (12½p) a bottle.

The jail entrance was to the left side of the Town Hall and beside that stood a harled house, gable end to the street as was often the style. The roadside portion was occupied by Gideon Johnstone as a bakery shop. This is the same Gideon who had his oven and house in the lane across the way. He had a bakery outlet in Kirkwall as well as Wick, as we see from his advert of 1842. Gideon retired from business in October of 1847 and the business was then run by his brother Thomas. The other portion of this building was the house of our Town Officer, Sandy Phimister, who gained access to his abode by a set of external steps between this property and the next. These two buildings were on the site now occupied by the Sheriff Court, which was built over the years 1862 – 1866. A footpath ran between the two buildings, past Sandy's stairs down toward the river, and between Jeanie Young's house and Donald Anderson's smiddy.

A Wee Diversion

Between the front of Jeannie Young's house and the jail yard wall was Jeannie's potato patch (famed for her early tatties) and Donald Reid's boatyard. Jeannie had only one leg and had taken up the profession of school mistress. She laid the educational foundations of many of Wick's learned and honourable sons, but as she grew older so her school diminished. "Wicker", writing many years later in the Ensign, paints a picture for us of the area and Jeannie.

"Poor Jeannie" he says "I can see her yet, hirplin on her crutch, after boys who had run through her tattie patch. She used to threaten them with, "I'll chist go for Sandy Phimister or Henry Osbourne an' hev ye a' locked up." Donald Reid the boat builder was not, at least to our younger generation, good natured, for when we boys made ships of the wood he laid down in the river, he would threaten us with all kinds of

Reduction in the Price of Bread.

GIDEON JOHNSTONE, BREAD AND BIS-
CUIT BAKER, WICK, PULTENEYTOWN,
KIRKWALL, has great pleasure in calling the
attention of the Public to the following announcement:—

KIRKWALL ESTABLISHMENT.—G. J. begs respectfully to tender his warmest thanks to the inhabitants
of this town and neighbourhood, for their kind support during the five years he has been in business
here. He has now the pleasure of intimating, that,
owing to an extensive purchase of Flour made by
him, at a moderate rate, for cash, he is enabled to
REDUCE the PRICE of the 4 lb. Loaf to 8d. Ready
Money, and 8½d. Credit. As every article in his line
will be laid in of the very best quality, he trusts to a
continuance of favours from his numerous Customers.

WICK ESTABLISHMENT.—G. J. also begs to state
that, for the accommodation of numerous Customers
in Wick and Pulteneytown, he will Bake, once a-
week, commencing this day, and each succeeding
Friday, a quantity of Loaves, made of Seconds Flour,
which he will be enabled to dispose of at 7d. the
4 lb. Loaf.

N.B.—All kinds of FANCY TEA-BREADS, and
SHIP and CABIN BISCUIT, regularly kept for
sale.

Orders from the Country punctually attended

16th September, 1842.

Gideon Johnstone's advert of Sept. 1842.
A 4lb loaf for a little over 3p.

27

Ah'll jist get Sandy Phimister 'till ye.

punishment. Neither would he let us throw stones on the roof of his shed, an innocent enough pastime (in Wicker's eyes). Between the smiddy, the boatshed and the river, was a fine open space for the "Ba" (this was the muckle yard) which was generally played after dinner. The good sense of, after dinner rest awhile, was not carried into practice by the youngsters, and apprentices, it was more a case of fifteen or twenty minutes for the tatties and herring, and forty minutes for "Hoose", ten or twelve a side, football being unknown in Wick back then."

I wonder about Wicker's statement that football was unknown in Wick in the middle of the 19th Century; had it died out? J.T.Calder in his History of Caithness mentions Ingram Sinclair amusing himself at football with some friends when he was shot dead by Earl George in the 1580s.

The Bridge Street Market

The weekly and other markets of this time were held in Bridge Street and from the bridge to High Street would be thronged on Fridays, which was market day. Country folk flocked into the town to sell and buy and, during the fishing season, it would be even busier. Cattle and horses for sale were not an uncommon sight and country produce of all kinds were displayed to the best advantage and in the most ingenious fashion. Many of the country folk would reverse their carts up against the east pavement, which was some two feet above the roadway. Having done this they would then turn the horse around in the shafts and place feed in the cart, thus making the horse comfortable. In the meantime, the goods for sale were arranged in the pavement side of the cart, "hey presto," a stall, all ready for business. Sarclet people were very well known for the quality and flavour of their haddies, half dozen in a bunch neatly tied by the tail found ready sale. Fresh, pouthered and salted butter, crowdie, cheese, sowan scones, white puddings, red puddings, as well as eggs in great quantity at 3d. a dozen(just over 1p.) Heather besoms and rashes were also on sale. Hens, ducks and geese in season were brought to market in sacks and sold live with much squealing as they passed from vendor to buyer. Apart from the weekly sales, there were special sales, or Fairs. These were, the first Tuesday after Palm Sunday, a variable date, June 24th. St. John the Baptist, and St. Fergus, or Fergusmass, which was the third Tuesday of November. These were very busy Fairs with lots of business transacted and considerable money in circulation. A good bit of the money no doubt found its way to the refreshment stalls and inns but the country folk would spend a goodly portion with the shopkeepers of the town. There were also travelling traders who not only attended the Fairs, but who also scoured the countryside. Famous men of their time were characters such as James Harper, Robbie Gibson, and Louie Bowman. The latter was a great character and well known throughout the county. He was a bit of a rhymester and would shout as he came,

"When Louie Bowman comes to town,

The rags are then in great renown,

When Louie Bowman gings awa'

The rags are sure to tak' a fa'.

He had the reputation of never taking no for an answer and many a wifie would find herself with "anither bonnie bowlie" she had never intended to buy.

Although prices varied from season to season, according to supply and demand, the prices in the mid 1840s were generally,

Flour 1/8d a stone (14lbs) app. 8p.

Quartern loaf (4lb) 1st Grade 5½d 2nd Grade 4½d app. 2p – 2½p

Eggs, fresh and definitely organic 3d per dozen app. a little over 1p.

Butter 8d per pound   app. 4p.

Beef 3½d per pound app. 1½p.

Beef Steak 5d per pound app. 2p.

These prices seem to us ridiculously cheap, but taking inflation into consideration, revaluation to today's values would be approximately;

One old penny   = 29p

One shilling(12d) = £3.50

One Pound   = £70

Five Pounds   = £350.

In those days, some of the Wick merchants carried on a considerable amount of wholesale trade, the smaller country shops drawing their supplies from the town and carriers came regularly to Wick from the villages around the county. A Mr Cruickshank came all the way from Helmsdale every Tuesday, carrying goods for shipment by sea and returning south with goods brought by sea for Helmsdale and as far south as Bonar Bridge. His starting point in town was David Gunn's shop in Bridge Street. Mr Cruickshank's son, John, worked with his father and, after Mr Cruickshank retired, John carried on the business. Both were highly thought of locally, being obliging and dependable.

From Lybster, itself a busy village, came Alexander Pryde, a butcher and grocer who visited Wick on Tuesdays and Saturdays. He came to buy for himself and other Lybster businesses and acted as a carrier for both steamer and wholesalers to the Lybster business community. Alex Waters was the other carrier for the Lybster area.

The other local carriers were;

Canisbay, Donald Sinclair, Friday.

Castletown, William Manson, George Murray, Tuesday and Saturday.

Dunbeath, Peter Bain, Tuesday and Saturday.

Latheron, Colin Dunbar and James Sutherland, Tuesday and Saturday.

Thurso, John Manson, Tuesday and Saturday.

Donald Weir, a well known egg merchant, visited the town every week and his trade was considerable. In the main season he would have two cartloads of eggs. Nearly all the traders took eggs in exchange for goods, but Donald Weir always paid cash for his purchases as he had ready buyers for his eggs.

John Macdonald of Louisburgh was a retailer of spirits, but also dealt in eggs. It is not recorded how many eggs he got for a bottle of Old Pulteney, but he certainly had a name for supplying good liquor. His shop was opposite Dr. Sinclair's house, which is now the Nethercliffe Hotel.

Characters

Wick had lots of regular visitors on Fridays, some who never missed a week and became very well known in the town, some were that wee bit special and stood out among the crowd. One such was a man called Alexander Bremner, much better known as "Tailor Lintie", who tipped along the pavement like a little bird fearing that the earth would open and swallow him up. His long, white oiled hair hung to his shoulders and he sported a very long but well groomed beard; he always wore a burnished top hat and his trousers were trimmed down each leg with an artillery stripe. Nowhere on his garments would you find a button, every orifice was secured with laces, hanging from all parts of his clothing. "Lintie" was a man fond of debate and always ready to back up his arguments with a scriptural reference. On one of his visits he was lamenting the increasing wickedness of the people, adding that hell was

Tailor Lintie.

"Robbie Scarlet".

now too small to hold them all. "How do you know that? he was asked. He swiftly answered, "Turn up Isaiah five at fourteen and there read, therefore hell hath enlarged herself! and what is that for, if not for the increase of wickedness?" He was a hard man to catch out and would never admit to being wrong.

Another worthy visitor was one, Donald Cask from Freswick, who was famous for his eccentric requests. On one occasion he rushed into Mr Kirk's shop on his way home and, planting his bonnet on the counter, said "Ah want twa pun o' trakle in a peiper bag an' clash 'id in 'e croon o' ma bonnid". Robbie Gunn, the assistant was speechless, history does not record if the request was ever fulfilled. Two pounds of treacle in a paper bag? what a thought! Especially in the crown of your bonnet.

One more character of that time is worthy of mention:– Robert Campbell, a native of Bower, known to all as "Robbie Scarlet." He joined a merchant ship at the age of thirteen, was pressed into the Royal Navy in 1794 and fought under Duncan at Camperdown, under Nelson at the Nile and was one of the eight hundred landed by Nelson at Aboukir Bay to assist the land forces of Sir Ralph Abercrombie. There he fought in three engagements in 1801. After his return he was discharged and that would have been enough for most mortals but not for our Robbie. He re-enlisted in the 23rd Regiment of the Line. At first this seems an odd choice, but it was in fact this regiment the Welsh Fusiliers, who led the attack at Aboukir Bay. Robbie served in the West Indies and was at the taking of Martinique. He was then sent to Spain with the regiment and fought under Wellington at Cuidad Rodrigo, Badajos, Albuera, Salamanca, (at which both of his sons were killed) and finally Toulouse. He was discharged from the army at the age of sixty four. Back home he deteriorated but at market days he would eagerly relive his days of glory with the shout, " Ah wis a hero afore ye wis born, an' ah'm a hero yit!"

There were many other "Worthies" around our town and county in those far off days and although today we find much amusement in their mannerisms and ways, the truth is that many of them had quite a rough time of it. Most of them were destitute, classed as paupers, and often dependant on a Saturday penny from the local shopkeepers and in spite of the Poor Law Board, set up in the mid 1840s, many depended on the generosity of others to survive. The herring was seasonal of course and after a poor season, although there was some alternative work, quarries, road mending etc., there really could be a long "winter of discontent" which would soon eat into any small savings and stores. We can only shudder at the knock on effect on the poor of the day. Our modern, much maligned "care society", makes such a difference to many of the "there but for the grace of God, go I" and we are, or should be, grateful for it.

With a little thought and imagination, it is easy to picture the scene in Bridge Street with all the bustle and crowds. The calls of the sellers, the noise of the livestock, the chatter and laughter of the adults and the shouts and squeals of the children as they dodged about between the stalls and the people: The dust of the dry day and the mud and puddles of the wet ones. The mixture of aromas, both pleasant and otherwise, and bad though some of the smells must have been they were surely less obnoxious and more organic than our modern day carbon monoxide outpourings. John Horne offers the following description of a Fergusmass Market.

"What a conglomeration of abominations was seen! What an amalgamation of sounds was heard! There stood a humble stall devoted to the sale of villainous gingerbread and sweeties. Here another, on which, lay in admirable confusion, quantities of glass beads, Shorter Catechisms, wicker baskets, horn spoons, the veracious history of George Buchanan, and melancholy ballads. What a mass of gaudily dressed lasses with be–mudded cotton stockings ; swaggering country blades ; obstreperous cows that were not to be controlled ; contumacious horses that would not be ruled! This, with the accompanying noise, dirt, confusion and jumble, constituted the Fergusmass Market."

After a time, and due to developments in Bridge Street, the Market moved into the High Street and along to what was to become, later in the century, the Market Square.

Back to the Shops.

The shop next along from Sandy Phimister's house had two or three steps up to the frontage. The interior was divided by a wooden partition with John Macgregor, Watchmaker on one side, and William Dunnett, Saddler, on the other.

John Macgregor was considered a crack hand at watches and, although advanced in years, was never away from the shop. The watches which he had on hand for repair or cleaning, were hung in rows, backs to the window. Gold watches were few and far between in the Burgh, but it was noticeable that Mr. Macgregor had more gold watches than any of the other three watchmakers in Wick and the one in Pulteney, thus proving that he had "the pick of the trade." It was a great attraction for folk to stand at his window and watch him at work, busy with the forceps or brushing up a wheel. Wick folk would tell you that if you took a watch in for cleaning, John would invariably say "och yer verge is broken", or "yer mainspring is gone my man", always a vital fault! Mr Macgregor was also contracted by the Wick Town Council to wind and maintain the town clock, which he did for many years. His son John jun. also worked in the shop but, tragically, died suddenly one day at work aged only thirty five. Mr Macgregor did not use any of the shop entrance for display, so Mr William Dunnett used the whole area to hang his goods, saddles, collars, harness, whips etc.etc. as many items as he could fit into the space and show to the public. He had the reputation of being an excellent salesman, mild spoken, and as persuasive as he was mild. He had a considerable business connection in Orkney and regularly visited his clientele across the Firth. His brother, Tom Dunnett, worked in the business with him.

Next along the street was a rather grand entrance which projected over the pavement with a balcony above, this was the entrance to The Caledonian Hotel. The landlord and mine host, Mr Alexander Leith, was contemporarily described thus, " a man just cut out for the business of a commercial hotel, frank, honest, jocular, homely and particularly mindful of his customers comforts!" – a high accolade indeed. The hotel was patronised by nearly all of the commercials and the "swells" who visited the town. The Caley was the start and stopping point for the Royal Mail coach, the clerk of which had a desk in the hotel bar and so the hotel had a large posting trade as well. On one occasion Lord John Hay, who was Member of Parliament for the Wick Burgh 1858 - 59, came out onto the hotel balcony to address the crowd gathered in the roadway and was considered quite daring.

We are now on the site that is built over today by Gunn's Footwear and Clothing Store, and Young, Robertson's Property shop. Back in the mid-19th century this area looked quite different. First was David Gunn, a licensed grocer, whose property was set well back from the roadway with a paved courtyard in front. This courtyard was used by local women as a kind of open market where they sold fish or other goods not sold by Mr Gunn. He also had a machine for the production of aerated water, this was placed in a shed to the rear of his shop and the process was quite an operation to watch. David Gunn's dress for this job was waterproofs, sea boots and a leather apron, with a receptacle for the bottle. When the tap was opened the water was driven into the bottle with great force and, when the bottle was full, the cork was driven home with a wooden mallet and wired down into place, all expertly handled by Mr Gunn, but a very wet business for him and all who dared watch. Mr Gunn's courtyard had yet another use; when the Royal Mail Coach was ready to depart, because there was insufficient room in front of the hotel, four or five men would lay hold and reverse the coach into the courtyard and so turn it round ready for its journey south. This coach always delivered the mail to the Caledonian Hotel and from there the mail was carried around to the Post Office, in Post Office Lane, nowadays Tolbooth Lane, Post Master Mr Craig. On one occasion a mail guard objected to the mail

John McGregor in his shop window working.

David Gunn's shop with its neat little courtyard.

In the 1840s and 50s this was the shop of Lachlan Dallas.

being carried round and ordered the driver to take the coach round to the foot of the lane. There was a bit more space here, but the time and skill required to make the tight turn in High Street was far outweighed by the ease of the turn in Bridge Street and so it reverted to the status quo.

A Nautical Diversion

The property in which Mr Gunn carried on his business was, before the Telford bridge was built, the birth place of Captain James Cormack. At this time the house faced into the Liach, or Loaning, what we now call Back Bridge Street. This lane led down to the little sands of Wick, now

Wind and Water!

Dᵣ GUNN AND CO.,

MANUFACTURERS OF

Ginger Beer, Lemonade, Soda Water, & Potass Water:

THE QUALITIES OF WHICH ARE NOT SURPASSED BY ANY IN BRITAIN—NOT EVEN BY THE FAMED "SCHWEPPE."

Let Connoisseurs compare.

The POTASS WATER is highly recommended by the Medical Faculty as an Effectual Cure for Rheumatism, and as a Superior Stomachic.

THE TRADE SUPPLIED.

SPORTSMEN taking SHOOTINGS in the NORTH will find it to their advantage to be Supplied by

D. GUNN & CO.,
BRIDGE STREET, WICK.

D. Gunn's Celebrated Soda Water and Lemonade can be had at the Exhibition Refreshment Rooms.

David Gunn's wind and water. "Better than Schweppe and would also cure rheumatism and stomach complaints.

Victoria Place etc. The rear garden of the Cormack house stretched across what is now Bridge Street and down to the edge of Kirk Lane. The Captain himself was a very interesting character; as a youth he served his time as a cooper with Mr William Bain, fish curer of Lower Pulteney, but the sea was his destiny. He took up the coasting trade, mainly the west coast of Scotland and Ireland. His first charge was the "Earl Gower", a smack of forty feet keel, later he bought the "Stormont" a smack of forty five feet keel and pursued the Wick to Leith trade. After the "Stormont" came the "Heroine" a ship of seventy-five feet keel and fitted out to carry up to thirty passengers. She was quite a swift vessel and one passage from Wick to Leith was accomplished in twenty hours and fifteen minutes. His last ship was a clipper that he had built at Montrose around the year 1845, eighty feet of keel and named the "Favourite." When he was appointed a harbour master at Wick in 1852 his trading days were over and the Favourite was sold.

The last shop of this line was that of Mr Lachlan Dallas, the Saddler. This was a neat two storied house with a castellated roof, considered by Wickers to be a pretty little building, and used by Mr Dallas as his business premises. Mr Dallas, assisted by his son James, specialised in fancy harness, manufacture and repair, the kind made from dressed and polished leathers with silver mounts and buckles. His window displays always excited much interest and admiration, mixed with envy from those who had to be content with plain leather, iron buckles, and maybe a length of twine to hold it all together.

Another wee diversion

The Dallas family lived out by the North Toll (at the north west corner of Robert Street and George Street described in the 1841 census as Hennyretta Street) and they had a pump well by their house; what an advantage in those days. In the fishing season the St.Fergus well at the south east corner of the Parish Church graveyard sometimes ran very slowly and it was a long job to fill up the kit or bucket, especially if the water had to be gathered in a cup as it came out of the spring. There were other wells around the Burgh but most would be in the same situation. At such times it was a very long wait, with maybe a dozen or more people waiting their turn. There were rules, unwritten, which governed the use of the well. If any person left the queue, for whatever reason, his or her place could not be regained. If anyone gave their place to another, the giver went to the back of the queue. A child could not keep a place for an adult. I dare say some rare squabbles erupted over interpretation of the rules. Instead of waiting for ages in the queue, some folk would walk out to the Dallas house and as a very great favour, would be allowed to "draw a fracht" from the pump. This well pump was kept locked at all times, so it was not possible to sneak a bucketful. In our modern times when water, both hot and cold, is so immediately at hand, it is difficult to appreciate the hardships faced by our ancestors over such a basic need. Were there ever "good old days?"

Mr Dallas' son James was a very well known figure in the parish. He was a good draughts player, a popular game at the time, and a violinist, a pupil of tutor, Hugh Warden. Another pupil of Hugh Warden was Dan

This is the site of what was once the St. Fergus well at the south east corner of the old Kirk yard.

JOHN O'GROAT JOURNAL, FRIDAY, SEPTEMBER 4, 1959

WICK'S LAST TOLL HOUSE IS DEMOLISHED

Wick's last toll house, at the junction of George Street and Robert Street, on the main road to the north, has been demolished. The Town Council will use the site for the erection of houses.

On the opposite side of George Street sre those attractive Council houses. The site was previously occupied by condemned property which was demolished. Eight houses will be built in the area where the Toll house stood, and they will be complimentary to those on the other side

GRAND
PROMENADE CONCERT
IN THE
TEMPERANCE HALL, WICK,
ON THE
Evening of Friday, the 11th inst.

THE promoters of this CONCERT intend that
the proceeds shall be exclusively applied for
the benefit of their old Townsman, Mr Hugh
Warden, who has for many years kept alive in
Wick the taste for Music, and the art of it. They
hope that by the kind co-operation of the Public
they shall realize a sum equal to their wishes.

PROGRAMME.
Part I.
Glorious Wellington.
Liverpool Hornpipe.
Song—'Jockie, the Gentle Shepherd.'
Royal Irish Quadrilles.
Catch—'Twas you, Sir.
Greig's Pipes.
PROMENADE.

Part II.
Selection of Scotch Airs.
Waltzes—Rosa and Lady Charlotte Bruce's.
Song—'When the Kye come hame.'
Cujus Animam, from Rosini's 'Stabat Mater.'
Paddy O'Rafferty.
Reel of Tulloch, with Variations.
PROMENADE.

Part III.
Selection of Highland Airs.
Song—'Irish Dan, his wife Nan, and their
daughter Ann.'
Auld Robin Gray, followed by 'Where will
bonnie Annie lie.'
Song—'Jock o' Hazeldean.'
Pibroch—'Breadalbane Gathering'—(Imitation
of Highland bagpipes.)
NATIONAL ANTHEM.
PROMENADE.

Refreshments will be procured in an Ante-Room.

Front Seats, 1s.; Back Seats, 6d.; Children under
12 Years, Half-price.

TICKETS may be had in Wick at the Office of
the *Northern Ensign*, and at Mr Kirk's Shop; and
in Pulteneytown at the *John O'Groat Journal*
Office, and at the Shop of Mr Wm. Sinclair,
Smith Terrace.

Doors open at Half-past Seven; Concert to com-
mence at Eight o'Clock.
Wick, March 8, 1853.

An advertisement for one of the many concerts in the Temperance
Hall. This one is for the benefit of Mr Hugh Warden, a respected music
tutor in Wick in the mid 19th Century.

Waters, who teamed up with James and the two were in great demand all over the parish, delighting dancers and audiences whenever the played.

We now cross the lane leading to Back Bridge Street and step into the first shop on the corner, Mr William Bell, Watch and Clockmaker. Over the door of his shop he had a clock, underneath which was written, Thirteen Minutes Faster Than Mean Time, indicating prime accuracy! To ensure his accuracy, he used a sextant, which must have been an unusual sight in Bridge Street. He also "had the Gaelic" and consequently a great proportion of the Highlanders who came to Wick for the fishing, gravitated to Mr Bell's shop if they owned or wanted to buy a time piece. As well as timepieces which, like Mr Macgregor farther along the street, he hung in rows in his windows, he adjusted compasses and, on foggy days during the season, he would be inundated with this work.

Mr Bell took over the maintenance of the Town Clock after Mr Macgregor's day. His apprentice was Francis (Francie) Cormack who, as a very special favour, would touch up your knife with a magnet, so that it would lift a needle. Later, Francie started up business on his own account over in Pulteneytown.

A Newsy Diversion

The Post Office as mentioned, was in Post Office Lane (Tolbooth Lane) and run by Mr Craig. When he died, Mr Bell was appointed Postmaster and the office moved to his shop in Bridge Street. At this time Mr Bell's assistant was Alexander Leith, who later moved to London and was one of the early members of The London Caithness Association. During the time of Mr Bell's reign as Postmaster, the Royal Mail Coach reached Wick at 10p.m. and left for the south in the "wee sma oors." This is now the time of the Crimean War 1854/1856. Mr Mackie who was editor of The Northern Ensign, the great rival paper to The John O' Groat Journal would, as a favour, get his south papers from Mr Bell as soon as they arrived. He would then take them round to his office in Stafford Place and, to a select group of cronies, would read out the news from the Crimea. His regular group was David Davidson, Willie Smith, William Rae and William Miller Junior with, occasionally, Malcolm Geddes, Andrew Colvin, and Charles Bruce. This was some thirteen years before the telegraph arrived in Caithness and the favourite source of Crimean news was Russell's Letters from the Crimea, published in The Times newspaper. Mr Bell's rapt listeners followed every part of the troop movements and battle reports, showing despondence at a set back and joy, even cheers at the report of a British advance or victory: no instant news from the front in your living room in those far off days. A great many men from our town and county fought and died in the Crimea and in every battle, Alma, Inkerman, Balaclava, Sevastapol as well as on ships of the Royal Navy as the monument at the North Head will testify, so news from the front was eagerly awaited. Mr Bell had the reputation of being a first class raconteur with an inexhaustible repertoire and a distinctive and infectious laugh.

Back to the shops

Above Mr Bell's shop Willie Smith had his tailoring shop, and, on the floor above that, his dwelling rooms, which were kept by his sister Annie. Willie was well known but did not enjoy a large patronage; he had a peculiar and rather brusque manner. A contemporary of Willie's said of him, " although intelligent, he was not given credit for the ability and knowledge he thought himself possessed of !" – beautifully put!

Willie was also an inveterate woman hater, due it was said, because he had had a marriage proposal rejected. He was however, very keen on debate and was one of the founder members of the Wick Mercantile Debating Society.

The next two shops along were both drapers; first George Craig, who took over this shop when the previously mentioned John Sandison moved premises. Next door to Craig's was Charles Bruce, brother of Provost William Bruce. When he gave up business in later years his shop was taken over by Hugh Loag continuing in the same trade. Mr Loag was in the habit of going south to make his seasonal purchases. The bales of goods that followed his return were piled up on the pavement edge in front of his shop, forming a veritable mountain. This of course became a dare, a challenge to the speed and skill of the local youngsters to run up and over the mountain, keeping a wary eye on the shop door through which Hugh Loag would rush, yardstick at the ready to deal out instant punishment. "Wicker" writing in the Northern Ensign in 1914 reminiscing about such an event wrote, " I've just put my hand round, I can't feel the mark now, but the memory is quite distinct."

At the end of the fishing season, and before the incomers returned to their own areas, it was the custom for many of the shopkeepers to hold an end of season sale, and it was this that inspired the now immortal slogan used by Hugh Loag when he advertised, "Hugh Loag's trousers, down again!"

The next premises in line was a shop with a small entrance porch on the style of, but smaller than, the Caledonian Hotel. This was Waters and

Mowat; they had the shop and the room upstairs as a drapery store and they were also fish curers, with a harbour and pier in the river. This harbour was approximately 100 metres to the town side of the north river pier, taken over after their time by John Baikie and so became Baikie's Harbour. The remnants of the pier are still visible in 2007 at low tide. (See page 54)

At one point, Messrs Waters and Mowat sat on a panel to look into the circumstances and conditions of all beggars in the community. One such was a man whose name was Jamie Harper Ross, an army pensioner of Irish extraction, who at some point had lost his left forearm, the stump was always wrapped in a white cloth and he might be seen with a fish or other goods pressed to his side by it, like a lever. John Horne, in his Caithness Originals describes the situation; Jamie was in a terrible pucker, afraid that he may be considered "an alien" and he addressed the following letter to Mr Mowat.

"To Mr Mode, merchant, Esq.— Mr Mode sir, I hope that you and Mr Watters will doo somethinge for me, James hurpur Ross at this meeting of beggars on tursday. I have that thrust in you Mr Mode that you will not see me nocked of and knoes I want the lift hand and has not the rite power in the rite one I am 13 yeare the first of April in Weeke an Poultney I have noe plase to goe too my wife belongs too the plase give me lave gintlemen to joge about my time on the erth is not longe anyway a man of tree score an tin so you too gintlemen I put my dipendance in you both to spake for poor James hurpur Ross. Gintlemen I hope you will mind me and I will mind you in my prayers." Whether Jamie was successful or not in his appeal, history sayeth not but, considering a letter of this strategic order, we think he deserved success.

When Waters and Mowat's gave up business, their shop was taken on by James Donaldson as a grocery business and Baillie Waters took the upstairs as his office and savings bank. Mr Donaldson soon outgrew this small premises and removed to Pulteneytown, where over the years the business changed to Gows and then Alexander and Keith.

Beside this shop was a property known as the Muckle Trance (big entrance) which is today a bookmakers. Above the door was a sign proclaiming Printing Office, this was on the first floor, and dealt with hand bills, bill heads, general jobbing and funeral letters which announced deaths and were circulated by the deceased's family, a practice which carried on up to World War Two. This business was not long lived and the premises were taken over by William Anderson who had it as his tailoring business. He was a musical man, violinist and singer, and was at one time precentor in the Muckle Kirk (Parish Church). One of his sons was named Charles Thompson Anderson, in

James Harper Ross.

10 *Kirk's Lane,*
Wick, Dec. 19th., 1910.

Sir,

My Wife, Robina Anderson, died here on Saturday Night at 8 O'Clock.

The favour of your presence to accompany her Remains to the Place of Interment, in the New Cemetery, on Wednesday, the 21st instant, at 3 O'Clock, P.M., is respectfully solicited by,

Sir,

Your obedient Servant,

David Rosie.

An example of the type of funeral announcement produced and sent to family and friends in times gone by. This one refers to my maternal great grandmother's funeral in 1910 well beyond the period of this book, but little changed over the years

compliment to the Rev. Charles Thompson who was minister of that congregation until the Disruption of 1843. Mr Anderson was quite a gifted man and a keen trout fisher who made his own sectional rods with brass ferrules as well as his own lines and flies. At one point he constructed a violin which played quite well. He was a staunch teetotaller and played the violin (not the one he made) and sang at the Temperance Society soirees and meetings, which were very popular and well attended.

Henry Taylor, a tailor and clothier, had the rest of the floor and had a large trade, employing several tailors. On the top floor yet another tailor, James Miller, plied his trade; he later moved to Aberdeen. Henry Taylor's eldest son, also Henry, worked in the business with his father. He had been to London and had served an apprenticeship learning cutting with the very well known tailoring house, Pooles of London. After his marriage he emigrated to Australia. During rain or snow, the "Trance" made an excellent shelter for the promenaders of Bridge Street. They would fill up the entire space, much to the annoyance of Mr Taylor and his clients. William Swanson, who would, many years later become the "Father" of the Wick coopers, would come in to Henry's workroom and read aloud to the working tailors from the Christian paper "Witness" and a few others. Willie read in a loud clear voice and one evening Henry remarked to a customer, "do you hear my chaplain? He is a fine reader, never sticks at a word no matter what the language, as long as it is printed in English letters – but ah! The Greek fair beats him" Then Henry laughed, and as usual, caught his left elbow with his right hand. Henry made a trip by a local vessel to Leith and Edinburgh on business and the trip went very well until the vessel was nearing Wick on the return journey. The wind rose and the vessel had to run to Cromarty and take shelter. It lay there for two weeks and Henry grew so impatient that he disembarked and set off on foot for Wick. It is not recorded how long he took but, as he arrived in Wick, he was just in time to see his ship sail into the bay. In the early 1850s the steamer fare from Wick to Leith was 16/- (80p.) for a 1st. cabin, 8/- (40p.) for a 2nd. cabin, children aged three to twelve, half price. Steamships available from Wick at this time were ships such as The Queen, Sovereign and Duke of Richmond; the local agent being James Bremner C.E.

A Sad Tale

Before Henry Taylor took occupancy of the Trance, he carried on his business in the Tibeth Vennel. At that time he had a John Sutherland working for him, a neat dapper little man, who fell in love with a young lady further down the Vennel. She, unfortunately, did not reciprocate his feelings and gave him no encouragement. John, finding all his advances repulsed, threw himself over the cliffs at Oldwick. He left a note under a stone at the point he went over addressed to his lady love but she never received it. The finder, after consulting with those around her, decided that it would only do harm. The note was neatly folded and addressed to Miss .... Wick. Oldwick Sept 16th 1827 it read;

Farewell my love since we must part, for surely you have broke my heart,

For in the deep here I do lie, God have mercy on my cry,

For, now, since the case was so, my heart has filled so full of woe

And rather than to pass you by, for you my love I'd rather die,

Farewell my love, here in the deep I do roll,

And God have mercy on my soul.

John Sutherland.

The unfortunate man's body was washed ashore a little further down the coast and was buried below high water mark.

This is the last property in Bridge Street as the next shop, which is today D.E.Shoes, had its entrance in High Street.

Before we leave Bridge Street, perhaps we could go back along the street and take a walk down Victoria Place and along the river towards the Camps. In February of 1916 a gentleman signing himself X.Y.Z. wrote a letter to the Ensign. He had been living in the south for over fifty years and had come home for a visit and was delighted with the improvements to the town centre, and especially the riverside, with its splendid green where formerly the river flowed from Rosebank to the Kirk yard wall, and, in times of high tide, almost up to St. Fergus well. He wrote the following:

"The young trees on either side of the river are a delight, especially to one who knew only one tree in Tolbooth Lane, and later the planting at Stirkoke, Scouthal being out of our reach. We never had a Sunday School picnic, money was scarce in the 1850s, and wages were low, men wore moleskin trousers and were not ashamed to be seen with patches at knee and seat. Yes, Wick was much improved, BUT, on walking down Victoria Place past the Zion Hall, what a forlorn and forsaken appearance greets the eye, a desolate, bleak, empty river, with broken down piers, and crumbling walls, instead of a hive of industry reaching from Parliament Close (beside Wetherspoons) out to almost the Kists (beyond North Baths). On a day when the boats average was 20/30 crans everybody was busy, hurrying about, herring being landed, filled into cran rings and poured into troughs, women and men busy, cleaning, packing, the silvery

1 Kirk Lane
2 Francis Quays
3 Willie Alexander
4 King Othos
5 Smiddy Coachworks
6 Dye Works
7 Muckle Yard
8 Jeannie Young
  & Donald Reid
9 John Gunn
10 Stafford Pl
11 Cock Lundies
12 Parliament Close
13 Parliament Sq
14 John Cleghorn's House
15 Shore Lane
16 Muckle Park
17 William Bain
18 George Auld
19 Tolbooth Lane
20 Old Town Hall
21 James Craig Tinsmith
22 Baptist Lane

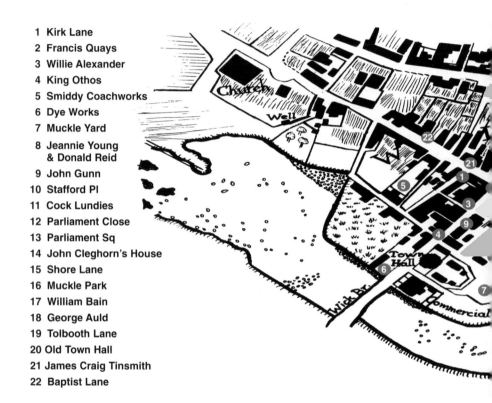

The Port and V

This is a rough plan of Wick town centre taken from a hydrographic map

Ar

y of Wick 1857

rt vicinity of Wick surveyed in 1839 and published in 1857 and redrawn by
ay

All that remains of Baikie's harbour pier are the stones on the extreme right.

Baikie's Harbour 2005, still a neat little area.

fish a pleasant sight but, no time for talking, work was the order of the day. Now, what a contrast.

Way back in the 1840s the first station on the river was that of Andrew Auld commonly called Andrew Oal. His boats, a goodly number, drew up in front and his troughs were usually well filled, with Andrew and his foreman, Davy Budge, here, there and everywhere directing, guiding and superintending the operations. Andrew was a town councillor and served as Dean of Guild for a time. He was a temperance man and when his employees needed refreshment they were served coffee, bread and butter.

William Bain's cooperage was in the building behind Mr Auld's station, his being a little further along and there was also a red herring kiln in the building. Mr Bain's two sons (see page 76) worked with him in the cooperage, I've truced a good many barrels put on the fire and started by son Alex, a recreation which got me out of bed at six o' clock on a winter morning, fine exercise for bringing up the muscles. One or two parts of the performance I could never quite master, I could never fill the grate from the spale bing, never could get enough in to complete the firing, neither could I place all the staves in the iron hoop, that was all done by Alex, and when all done I got the hammer and driver, for the life of me I cannot remember the right name for that tool, one end of which was placed on the hoop, and the other struck with the hammer as the striker goes round the barrel. There used to be a saying "I'll go roond ye lek a cooper goin' roond a barrel" These were the happy days of life, neither care or sorrow, but we did not know it then.

William Bain had his trough out on the jetty and George Simpson had his at the other end, Mr Simpson was also a rope maker. Next came George Sinclair's station, a very elaborate area and kept in splendid condition. He also had a station at Staxigoe, and was considered to be a "great swell." The next station was William Corner, and then Dannie Quoys, and then Bremner's, he was known more often as "Black King", his dwelling house and cooperage being in the building facing the river. Next to him was John Kirk's followed by Waters and Mowat, which became John Baikie's, his house was on the roadside opposite and there were some cowsheds and some smaller houses. Mr Baikie's house was easily recognised as the flagstones at his door were always neatly black leaded. (In modern terms we are a little before the foot of Scalesburn.)

Next along was the harbour of Captain Alexander Cormack, a fine roomy harbour and accessible by boats long after the tide had gone from the river harbours. The Captain's house was against the brae, with a platform at the back. (I wonder if this was the building which used to be just at the "turn" of Scalesburn. It was still there in the author's youth

Ware's harbour, once such a busy little place. Years ago this was a shingle bottom, nowadays littered with boulders.

The quay at Wares harbour, still in good shape after all those years.

and had a platform from the upper storey which linked across to the Scalesburn roadway, with a set of spiral steps which led down to ground level.) Our writer goes on,

"he was the very epitomy of an old sea captain, carrying a swell walking stick with a carved ivory head. He had an odd way of doing business, if any of his men needed an advance he would write a note thus; Please give to the bearer, Donald Mackay five shillings sterling, signed Alexander Cormack. The bearer would then take the note to a certain shop and the shopkeeper would pay out the money and file the Captain's note. This would build up to quite a number, but the Captain would make one of his rare appearances in the town and honour his debt. His son Alexander's hobby was sailing and he owned a few yachts, priding himself that he could beat any boat sailing into Wick bay, his boats were always immaculate.

Sandy Sinclair's harbour came next; a small harbour, but deep, with a slipway. Willie Falconer had his curing station there and his boats also used Sandy's harbour. On one occasion James Bremner C.E., now shipping agent, had a dispute with the Pulteney Harbour people and transferred his business to Sinclair's harbour. Here he erected a tripod crane for lifting heavy goods ashore from the bull boats (open, undecked barges) to the waiting carts and the passengers were landed or shipped from the slipway. This was a great time and the Wick-side folk were delighted hoping this would continue but the road from the Camps to Sinclair's harbour got into such a terrible muddy condition that the passengers got up in arms against it, and the upshot was that James Bremner moved back to Pulteney. About this time a bull boat, laden with goods, got washed from its moorings as it waited for the tide and was thrown on to the Odd, a complete wreck (approximately where the north river pier is now). John Mackay, a worthy of Wick commonly known as Jock Taty, was one of the men in charge of the boat and he was drowned, much to the sorrow of the community. John was a fine figure of a man, though rather weak of mind. He used to call into Mr Rae's shop, and, would say, "Mr Rae I want a pair of side combs for my sister Jessie." "What price Jock?", Mr Rae would ask. "A nice pair," would be Jock's reply. Mr Rae would then begin to take a box down. "No, no, Mr Rae, not that box, the flat box" said Jock. "Ah " said Mr Rae, "the ones in the flat box are sixpence:" to which Jock would reply, "weel weel, mind I want a nice pair, so you just show them to me." Jock would get the box onto the counter and begin to pick a pair, fumbling for his money at the same time, then, having settled on a pair, would lift them up, plank two pence on the counter, and run out of the shop for all he was worth, laughing loudly. The next time, Mr Rae wanted a job done, Jock would do it with all his might and main and, when finished, would say "weel, Mr Rae, that pays for the side combs." I dare say it did!

The last station on the north side, was that of Alexander Wares, a small harbour only big enough for a few boats. He also had a cooperage, a store and a kiln and his house was above, up near the roadway."

All of these harbours changed names from time to time as people gave up business, died or sold on: thus this last harbour is often referred to as Levack's harbour, as he was the first man to work it. What a sight it must have been to see the whole northern shoreline so alive and so busy and with a resident population along the whole length of the shore.

The High Street

The first shop we come across in the High Street as we head towards Market Place is that of William Bruce (now DE Shoes but back then the door was in the High Street). This was known as Provost Bruce's shop and he was known for the quality of the cloth which he stocked in single and double widths, known then as narrow and broadcloth, and in qualities such as West of England, a medium weight tweed with a soft handle, which also tailors rather well. An indication of the range of cloths which he stocked can be seen by his advert of November 10th. 1853, an astonishing variety. How he fitted it all into those premises is a mystery. He also had a name for ladies "Filled Plaids", a fashion which died out by the end of the century but, at the time, was an essential part of a young lady's wardrobe when she married.

Mr Bruce was well known for his placid ways, no matter how difficult the customer; he would show length after length of cloth until either the customer was satisfied, or rejected his stock. If the latter occurred, he still remained calm, smiling, and courteous. Some of the young blades of the town decided to test his patience and temper. One of them entered the shop and became the classic difficult customer rejecting all that was shown to him. Mr Bruce remained his usual courteous self, eventually the young man pointed to the very first cloth that had been shown and planting a shilling coin (5p.) on the counter said "a shillingsworth please." Mr Bruce, without a comment, took the coin, placed it on the corner of the cloth, cut carefully round it, wrapped the piece of cloth in paper, handed it to his tormentor, thanked him for his business, then with a passing comment on the weather, dropped the coin into his till. Mr Bruce had two spells as Provost, first 1836-37 and then 1839 to 1843. he and his brother Charles had a great interest in history and their papers and transcriptions are, today, lodged with North Highland Archive in Wick.

The Provost's shop had a window facing into Bridge Street; this window had an iron bar across it, projecting about a foot from the glass as a protection. This was a favourite corner for the loungers of Wick who leaned against the iron bar resting their arms on it. There were usually five or six of them, smoking or chewing tobacco and decorating the pavement with the result, a perfect nuisance to all the passers by. In front of the shop, in the High Street there was quite a wide pavement as there is today and a little to the East and out on the cobbled road was the Market Cross, made of rounded boulders (Wickers would call them shore bools) set into the roadway.

Two Gundy stalls were here (for the uninitiated, Gundy is a chewy toffee,

NEW ARRIVALS
OF
CLOTH, GENERAL DRAPERY, HATS, &c.

WILLIAM BRUCE

BEGS to intimate the return of CHARLES BRUCE from the MARKETS and MANUFACTURING DISTRICTS in the South, with a Large and Well Selected STOCK of GOODS Suitable for the Season, which having been Carefully Selected, and Purchased upon the Most Advantageous Terms, will he hopes merit a Continuation of that Patronage so liberally bestowed.

The following is a List of his principal Purchases:—

SUPERFINE WEST of ENGLAND and YORKSHIRE CLOTHS, in the Most Fashionable Colours.

WITNEYS, BEAVERS, PILOTS, SIBERIANS, and MILLED CLOTHS, suitable for Overcoats.

BLACK and COLOURED DOESKINS, CASSIMERES, and SATARRAS, in Great Variety.

A Choice Assortment of SCOTCH and ENGLISH TWEEDS.

VESTINGS—in VELVET, PLUSH, SATIN, BROCADE, MOIRE ANTIQUE, VALENCIA, QUILTING, and other Fabrics.

VELVETEENS, VELVETS, MOLESKINS, LINEN CHECKS, GAMBROONS, GRANDRILLS, JANES, &c.

DRESS MATERIALS—in MERINOES, COBURGS, LUSTRES, AUSTRALIAN CRAPES, CIRCASSIANS, BAYADERES, WINCIES, and GALA TARTANS.

PRINTS, REGATTAS, GINGHAMS, DRUGGETS, and DERRIES.

SHAWLS, in LONG and SQUARE CASHMERE, CASHMERE D'ECOSSE, INDIANA, TARTAN, and a Variety of Fancy Styles.

WITNEY, BATH, ENGLISH and SCOTCH BLANKETS.

MARSEILLE, VICTORIA, and TOILET QUILTS; WHITE and COLOURED COUNTER-PANES; CARPET COVERS.

BROWN and BLEACHED LINEN and COTTON TICKS.

LINEN and COTTON SHEETINGS, Plain and Twilled.

BED and TABLE LINEN, TOWELLING, FURNITURE STRIPES and PRINTS.

IRISH and SCOTCH LINENS.

WHITE and GREY SHIRTINGS; RAILWAY, JANE, and HEAVY STRIPES.

WELSH, SAXONY, SILESIAN, MEDIUM, and SWANSKIN FLANNELS, all Widths.

BLUE FLANNELS and PLAIDINGS.

ENGLISH and SCOTCH SERGES and PLAIDINGS.

A Well Selected Assortment of GENTLEMEN'S UNDERCLOTHING, in LAMBS' WOOL SHIRTS, DRAWERS, and HOSIERY.

GENTLEMEN'S SHIRTS, in LINEN, COTTON, and FANCY STRIPES, Of the Newest Shapes and Designs.

SHIRT FRONTS, COLLARS, and STUDS.

(Shirts Made to Order.)

STUFF, SATIN, FELT, and YACHTING HATS.

An Extensive Variety of CAPS, in the Newest Styles and Materials.

A Large Stock of SATIN, SILK, and SPUN HANDKERCHIEFS.

ALBERT, NAPOLEON, ARIEL, and BEAUFORT TIES.

SILK, CLOTH, CASHMERE, and BUCKSKIN GLOVES.

(Also Agent for) ROUGH'S DUNDEE KID GLOVES.

BALMORAL, ATHOL, and GLENGARRY BONNETS.

FINGERING and WHEELING YARNS.

MUFFLERS, BRACES, WEB and LEATHER SHOES, &c.

W. B. would call special attention to his CLOTHS and HATS, which have been purchased decidedly Cheap, and will be sold on the smallest remunerating Profits.

Wick, October 1853.

William Bruce advertises his new autumn range of cloths, gloves, hats etc. How did he fit this impressive stock into his shop?

sometimes flavoured with cloves, not much made these days). Nelly had one stall and Chirsty ran the other. They worked along side one another for a long time then one day, for an unknown reason, they fell out and after a big "washing of dirty linen" in public, Nelly moved her stall across the road and set it up in front of the coal yard by the old town hall steps. This in modern terms, would be between Mackay's Stores and Lloyds T.S.B. Nelly only sold her Gundy to people she liked or to strangers; anyone seen buying from Chirsty was immediately removed from her list, and she did remember. Mr Mackie, Editor of the Ensign, did or said something which, unbeknown to him, offended Nelly and she refused to serve him. He got a youngster to buy some for him but this was spotted by Nelly who treated the editor to a lashing from her very sharp tongue. She was quick witted as well as sharp and more than a few Wickers found that to their cost. One youth said, " Nelly, yer gundy's dirty". "Aye" replied Nelly, "Ah made id chist for yer mooth". On another occasion a youth said, " Ah'll gie ye a penny for a stalk Nelly"; to which she replied, "No, tho' ye'd gie me a shilling, ye oogly lookin moniment, off wi' ye or ah'll gie ye as muckle as 'll keep ye in e' hoose for a week!" Nelly and Chirsty never spoke again, although they may have privately forgiven each other. Chirsty died in 1856, so Nelly had the monopoly on the gundy sales. Around this time she became frustrated with the cheek she received from one of Wick's urchins and hit him with her stick. She was charged and brought to court where she got off with a deferred sentence. After this escapade she moved her stall, which was two soap boxes laid side by side, back across the road to the steps in front of Mr Colvin's shop, in Stafford Place. Nelly, real name Ellen Bruce, died aged eighty in March of 1868. The Ensign reported that, "recently Nelly had become rather frail, but it was not more than ten days since she was at her post, dispensing gundy to her favourites, and vowing vengeance on certain individuals who had offended her."

John Horne in his " Caithness Originals" wrote, " She was very frail in her later years, but held to her post bravely. Ten days before her death she went home "clean done" and took to her bed. The threatening, scolding figure was never seen again on the spot which had known her so long, and the name of Nelly Gundy became the label of a memory."

A man called Moses Jacob had a stall in this area as well and in the evenings sold by auction all manner of goods, new and used, by the light of a sputtering lamp. Moses actually had a shop on the King George IV Bridge in Edinburgh dealing in all sorts of articles. He had a son, Isaac, who came to Wick with him and attended school here. Moses was quite a character, with a ready wit, and never short of an answer. He was called as a witness in court and, when asked to state his name, replied in a loud voice "Moses Jacob". " What?" said the court official in a sort of

Ellen Bruce, a.k.a. Nelly Gundy, who added character to the Streets of Wick for many a year.

off taking manner. The answer came back in an even louder voice "Moses Jacob, I could have a name like yours if I wanted, but I'm damned if I'd have it!"

It seems that Provost Bruce had a habit of having a chat with Moses Jacob, whose stall was outside his shop. At the end of one season the stallholder gave the Provost his address in Edinburgh and suggested that if Mr Bruce was ever in the capital he might like to look him up. Not too long after that Mr Bruce had occasion to go to Edinburgh and, having some time to spare, resolved to call on Moses. The address turned out to be in a very desirable area of the city and it was with a feeling of doubt that the Provost went up the steps and pulled the brass bell knob of an elegant Georgian house. The door was opened by a parlour maid in cap and apron who showed him into a handsomely furnished room. A few minutes later in walked Moses in dapper city dress. Moses advanced toward the Provost and asked "to whom do I have the honour of speaking?" Provost Bruce explained who he was and recognition dawned in the eyes of Moses. "Ah, yes" he exclaimed "you're the man who has that wee shop behind my stall in Wick!"

In August of 1846 James Bremner launched a prototype lifeboat that was propelled by two paddle wheels in the centre of the craft and operated by eight men. With Mr Bremner himself at the tiller the boat paddled out to the mouth of the bay and back to the harbour. The speed was good and the vessel quite worthy but the effort required to work the paddles was immense and the men were soaked with perspiration. The boat was never recognised by the Wick Lifeboat Service and was eventually bought by Sir George Dunbar. He took it to Ackergill and it lay on the shore below the tower for a long time. Moses Jacob came across it on one of his peregrinations and made an offer for it to Sir George, which was accepted. A few days later Moses arrived at Ackergill with a hurley (a hand cart) and set fire to the boat, reducing it to ashes. He then sifted the ashes removing all the copper fastenings which he disposed of later in the south at a reported profit of 150%.

At the back of Provost Bruce's shop and across the way, now the Back Bridge Street Club, Willie Oal had a butchers premises. At this time, butchers had a pretty free hand and Willie slaughtered on the premises. His property was somewhat primitive, one of the early buildings of the town with a turf or divot roof, and the windows were simply holes in the wall covered with shutters at night. Willie killed at intervals and a few days beforehand, he would go round his clients booking orders for particular joints and cuts, informing them of the day the meat would be ready. Willie Rugg was the man who fetched the beast in from the country, as he did for most of the butchers. He was a short stout man, of

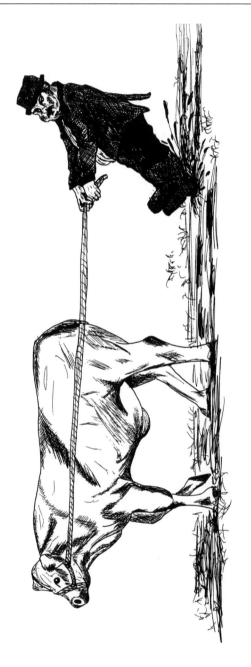

Willie Rugg, an original Wick cowpoke.

whom it was said, "he had grand understandings and boots big enough for them." His performance fetching the beasts was something to be seen and quite often he would be dragged, heels dug in against the pull of the cow, from the Muckle Kirk to Bridge Street but he never let go until the animal was delivered to the butcher. Willie Oal always dressed in a frock coat and top hat, both of which had seen top fashion a few times. There was once an Oal's Close off Louisburgh Street across from the top of Oag's Lane, whether it had anything to do with our Willie Oal we may never know.

Now we are in Stafford Place and the first two shops were occupied by Purves and Brown, they were grocers and drapers. After them the drapery shop was taken by a Robert MacLean who came from Hawick and ran a ladies outfitting business. He did not stay in Wick long and the shop was then taken by James Robertson. The grocery business was bought by an Edinburgh man, R.H.Colvin, who was assisted in the business by his brother Andrew. Mr Colvin, tragically, died in March of 1850, aged only thirty two, leaving a widow and three children and then Janet, the eldest daughter, died aged six in July of the same year and Andrew carried on the business on behalf of the family and worked up a good trade. Then James Johnston, a brother of Mrs Colvin, came to take part in running the shop. Later Andrew tried his hand at farming, but with little success. Mrs. Elizabeth Johnson died in October of 1868 aged only forty seven.

The end premises were that of William Rae, printer, bookbinder, bookseller, and stationer. He was born in 1811 in Gillock and began his working life as an apprentice cabinet maker with Mr John Bruce in Lower Pulteney. Once he had served his time he spent a year in Kirkwall, before moving to Glasgow where he took every opportunity to advance his education. It was here with Mr William Levack that they conceived the idea of an association of Caithness men, which became that worthy body, The Glasgow Caithness. In 1839 Mr Rae returned to Wick and began business for himself. At one point he ran a reading room and started a book club where the members paid an annual subscription of 21/- (£1.05p). At the end of each year the books, having done the rounds of the members, were sold and the proceeds split between the group. This was given up when Mr Rae took over the Northern Ensign in 1853 with Mr Mackie staying on as editor. Eventually Mr Rae owned the whole of Stafford Place and used a substantial part of it for his business. Mr Rae was, later, Provost of Wick for twelve years from 1874 to 1886 and was also Chairman of the Harbour Trust and involved with many other local groups.

Under Mr Rae's shop, Alexander Gunn and his brother David, known

This photograph of Stafford Place was taken c.1875, showing The Northern Ensign Office, Sinclair Bros Grocers and James Manson, Draper. The basement premises at this time was occupied by Archibald Campbell, Baker. Photograph by kind permission of The Wick Society, Johnston Collection.

locally as Bicker, had their oven and bakery shop. These basement premises have all been filled-in and the steps and railings that formerly fronted the building have been removed and the pavement levelled. Today no trace remains. The whole side of the street, from Bruce's shop to Rae's, was in the fishing season, taken up with stalls, weight and height machines and other fancy goods. It is nice nowadays, on a Saturday morning, to see the stalls of the modern day traders carrying on the old traditions in the same area (knowingly or not).

At the side of Stafford Place was Cock Lundie's Close, sometimes referred to as Lundie Close. I wonder if our modern name of London Close is a corruption of the older name? This close now no longer really exists, but in its heyday must have been quite a place. Our friend "Wicker" writing of the area as it was in the 1840s says, " Cock Lundies Close was one of the lions of the Royal Burgh, I'm not sure of the name of the proprietrix, I think it was Sutherland. I knew her quite well, and also her mansion, I was never inside but often on top of the wall. When I knew it, it was without a roof, the lady lived in the ground floor with the first floor serving as the roof. The stair was still there, and the floor was covered with some waterproof material. I do not think this was a very satisfactory solution. Her neighbours in the close were folk well known in the Burgh. Mr Robert Hay and Mr Alex. Snuff, at the bottom, Mr John Crory, Miss Kitty Groat, the Plowman family, Pierce the showman and champion boxer, who got married in Wick, he and his wife had a short honeymoon, they were married, I think on a Thursday, and by Saturday he was back in the ring challenging all to fight him. There were others who were birds of passage."

In the 1851 census no less than thirty nine people, of eleven residences, lived in the close. Cock Lundies must be a very old name as by 1851 it was known as London Mans Close, and the old house occupied by Mrs Sutherland was giving concern as to its condition according to the discussions of the Town Council.

James Sinclair, meal dealer, had the next shop (Mrs. Sutherland's property) and his brother Danny helped him. To his business he added hide dealing and tallow melting, the latter being carried out by John Crory. Everyone knew the day when the tallow melting took place as it could be smelt from Kirk to Shore.

Above Mr Sinclair's and reached by an outside stairs, was a joiner shop and when it was given up it was taken by Lachlan Swanson and his two sons as a tailoring shop. Lachlan was a tall man but both his sons were below average height. They lived over in Pulteney and always walked to the shop in company when the contrast in heights was quite marked. Lachlan was a local man who had lived in the south for some time before coming back to his native town. After a time they moved back south.

Alexander Waters, Butcher, had the next shop on the corner of the Market Place, and round the corner was another Butcher, William Steven, who was assisted in the shop by his son, also William, while James, the eldest, ran a butcher shop in Lower Pulteney. This is all on the site of the Highland Council offices. This area was known then as the "Shambles", a term used to describe an area where butchers set out stalls to sell their meat.

Next to Steven's shop was the Market Shed, where the fish wives and others laid out their wares for sale and, like the butcher meat, these were open to the air and any pollution from people or insects. Did it do anyone harm? Maybe we've swung too far the other way and lost some of our natural resistances. The house next to the shed was occupied by a John Fraser who hailed from Inverness and was a shoemaker and a first rate hand at fine work. He was employed by Mr William Mowatt. Mr Fraser once walked from Inverness to Wick, a distance then of 120 miles. He said that he had left Inverness at six o'clock on the Friday night and arrived in Wick at six o'clock on the Saturday evening. He at once earned the sobriquet "supple flank" by which he was known for the rest of his days in the town. Joey Gilbertson, known as the ironbound cooper, lived in the other part of the house. He made pails, kits and leepies; the latter a measure used for potatoes. At this time he was Tacksman of the Town Customs and was quite "active" in pursuing the same; he especially would "look after" anyone who took a fowl, goose, cheese, or piece of meat to town and took it to a shop to be weighed instead of coming to him and paying their money. On Fridays and other market days, he had a show of his goods on the old town hall stairs and took orders for churns, meal barrels etc.

The Market Place was the area where all the Cheap Johns or Cheap Jacks assembled with their various stalls. One of them sold rock at a penny a lump; he called it Californian Gold, and so he was known as California. At the time of the Hill Markets, some of the shows would stay on for a while and set up in the Market Place.

A little on The Hill Markets

In the beginning, the Hill Markets were held on what was known as the Hill o' Week, on the area known to this day as Market Hill. These were great occasions where considerable business was transacted; horses, cattle, and sheep were bought and sold and also hiring of servants etc. At Market Hill, the layout of the market was, generally, a caravan or two along the top and then two rows of stalls or tents, extending for two to three hundred yards, with a wide avenue between, where the throngs of people gathered. At the lower end, and outside the stall lines, the animals were exposed for sale. There were refreshment tents, sweetie and other stalls, and all the fun of the fair; strong men, fat ladies, giants, dwarves, as well as curiosities, and usually a menagerie. Batty's Royal Menagerie were frequent visitors to the county and would attend such markets and when in town, filled the whole Market Place with feeding times a great attraction. The John O' Groat Journal reported in May of 1853 that a Wick boy by the name of Bain visited the menagerie, approached too close to the lioness in her den and began to torment the beast by spitting tobacco juice into her eye. The lioness, taking full advantage of the proximity of the boy, suddenly caught him with her claws, cutting him severely across the head. Fortunately, Dr. Sinclair was quickly on the scene and treated him or, as the "Groat" put it, "adopted the necessary remedies." Batty's show also had a band which gave afternoon and evening concerts.

Dr Sinclair

Later the Hill Market was held out at the end of the North Head, on what was then a piece of rough uncultivated ground. It went from strength to strength and became a very important fair. Later still in the century it was moved to the riverside, first on the old haugh site and latterly to the riverside, but it never regained its former glory and faded away.

Back to the Market Place

Beside Josey Gibertson's shop a lane led down to the river and on the next corner, (in modern terms, approximately The Alexander Bain's bar area,) was Alexander Levack's premises, a butcher's shop, stables and slaughterhouse; he was reckoned to have the best of the local trade. Down past his area was Bruce the blacksmith. Mr Bruce was a little man who, when out of the smiddy, wore a leather apron and a top hat and had a reputation for his lock picking skills. If a key was lost or locked inside Mr Bruce was first call and sure to effect an entry, a quiet smile usually followed with the remark "there you are then". Only once was he beaten, by a trunk with a patent spring lock. When the trunk was forced, he examined the lock, and declared, " no man on earth could pick that." He was a very mild tempered man and, if anyone made a rude remark to him, his usual reply was simply "weel weel."

We are still in the area now occupied by the well known public house, The Alexander Bain; all those years ago it looked so different. Across from Levacks was the premises of John Swanson and George Cormack, joiners, carpenters and cabinet makers. Mr Cormack lost the use of his legs and was bedridden for many years, however he had a rack fitted up for his tools beside his bed and did small carrying work for a long time. Mr Swanson had been very active in the local branch of the Chartist movement, the aims of which were laid out in the Groat of April 28 1837 as

1. Manhood Suffrage.

2. Abolition of property qualification.

3. Equal electoral districts.

4. Vote by ballot.

5. Payment of M.P.s

6. Annual parliaments.

Further along was Parliament Close, another lane described as one of the Wick Lions, not as fashionable as Cock Lundies but running it close, the roofs of the latter were turfed and the former slated. Cock Lundies was on the brae head and the Close ran down to the river. Up on the street and next to the joiner shop was a Public House. When the owner first made application for a licence he was asked, "are you married sir?" when he replied in the negative, he was asked, " who will look after the house?" he replied "me and my sister Maggie." Needless to say, in true Wick style, he was forever known as Sister Maggie.

Mrs Bruce, pastry cook, grocer etc. had the next shop with the house above. In one of her windows she displayed samples of her skills in pastries and sweets, while in the other she usually had a display of crockery. Her husband was a blacksmith and had his smiddy at the head of a little lane opposite. Aeness Craig had a joiner shop in the other end of the building.

Now we are in Parliament Square and may regain our bearings. In the left corner of the Square was John Sutherland's public house; and a narrow lane ran down from here to the river, a very handy lane if you did not want the town to know that you had been in the house. This lane housed a property which in former times was known as Pesleys Tenement, which was at one time owned by the parents of the infamous Pirate Gow. Sutherland's became a sort of club for the fish curers, it being handy for the shore, so they would meet here to discuss the goings on in the trade. One day, after getting through the business and relaxing socially, a few of the inner circle began making up little rhymes about

Today, this is all that remains of the lane which led down from John Sutherland's public house in Parliament Square.

each other. One Eben Miller, who lived in a grand house with pillars at the door, made a telling rhyme about one of his colleagues, who swiftly replied;

Eben Miller you'll sit there 'till you drink all your siller,

And leave nothing to your wife but a Corinthian pillar.

It was customary for many fishermen to have a "Moarnin" (morning dram) sometimes converted to a brose like substance with the addition of a spoonful or two of oatmeal. I cannot vouch for the taste but, if you feel brave, have a go!

It has often been said locally that Parliament Square was so named because King James the Sixth held a Parliament here in 1589, when he signed the charter raising Wick to the status of a Royal Burgh. It is a lovely romantic story but, sadly, not true, King James was never in Wick; 1589 was his marriage year, when he married Anne, daughter of the King of Denmark and Norway, and of course he did not have his troubles to seek with his own nobles. In fact once he became James the First of Great Britain, he was never again in Scotland let alone in Wick. The original Charter of 1589 is now held once more, in Wick, in The North Highland Archive; it was signed in Edinburgh. A more likely reason for the name is that the original Provost's house was in the square, still is, but mostly built over, and this is where the old time functionaries had their meetings, or where they met to "parley."

From this part of High Street we have a big jump to the next property which was Mr Cleghorn, the Ironmonger's house, opposite the bottom of Shore Lane. The property now houses the Citizen's Advice Bureau. The only property after this was a store belonging to Mr George Simpson: we are now at the Camps.

On the opposite side of the road, there were three houses, the first John Wares, fisherman, whose windows faced onto the river, but his door was at the back reached by an entry between this and the next house occupied by a Mrs Sutherland. The end house was that of Charles Arnold who had a garden at the side reaching the foot of what was then Shore Vennel, (Shore Lane). We will meet Mr Arnold later in the High Street. All of this area has been rebuilt over the years. The house at the top of the Shore Vennel, known as Mount Hooly, corrupted from Holy Mount was the home of Provost Bruce, who grew several kinds of fruit trees against the garden walls. At this time there were only five small houses at the top west side of the lane, none at all in the lower half and the whole area from Louisburgh to High Street was an open area known as The Muckle Park, or The Hall Park, as the Temperance Hall stood at the head of it. After the disruption of the Church of Scotland in 1843 the folk who had left to start The Free Church had nowhere to worship and often met in the Temperance Hall. In more clement weather they met in the park. Rev. Thompson had a portable pulpit, something after the fashion of a sentry box, and his congregation sat on the grass on temporary trestles, or brought their own stools. Later this congregation built their own chapel down in Kirk Lane and then in the 1860s built Bridge Street Church.

The Muckle Park

This whole area is the subject of an ancient charter and was owned by the church; this was, of course, before the reformation of 1560. On the 14th day of February 1503, Andrew, Bishop of Caithness, disponed to Alexander Brysbane that part of this ground lying to the east, afterwards known as Brysbane's tenement, the western part being known as Vicars Tenement. The full charter is reproduced in J.T. Calders' History of Caithness.

In 1881 excavations took place at the foot of The Muckle Park, clearing a site for buildings to be erected by Provost Rae. These excavations were being carried out about six or seven feet above the level of High Street. The Northern Ensign reported;

In the course of excavation workmen came upon the remains of an old house, lying nearly parallel to the High Street, and having a strip of causeway in front of it. Everyone was surprised to see a house reveal itself where that reliable authority, the "oldest inhabitant" never saw a house, or suspected one to be. The length of the building was about thirty five feet, and the breadth about twenty feet. The stones used in the construction were generally above the size of those used in very old buildings, and were built with clay, their outer surfaces being what is termed, quarry faced. The height of the remaining portion of the front, and gable walls is about three feet, that at the back being four feet. In the front wall were a door and two windows, while in the back there was only a door, but considerably wider than that at the front, and gave access to a court or area behind. A thick stone wall or partition divided the building near the centre. The causeway mentioned was found to be almost level with the present run of High Street, which is fully two feet under the level it stood at thirty years ago. The workmen found the interior filled with the upper portions of the walls and gables and other rubbish. Over this lay a mixed deposit, composed principally of quarry chips and "tirrings" from the quarries which are said to have been worked in its vicinity. Over this deposit was spread a considerable layer of good black mould, evidently taken from the upper end of the park where the Temperance Hall now stands.

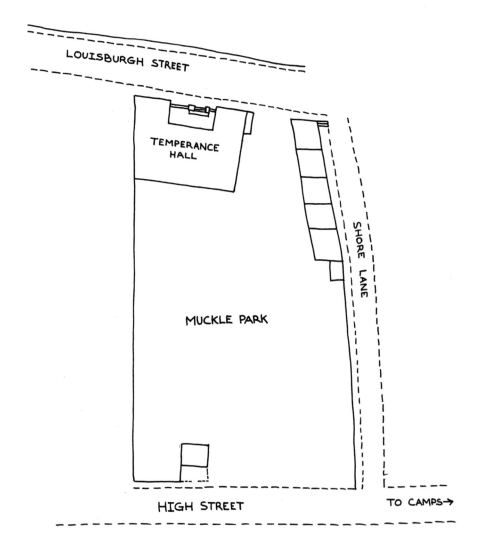

MUCKLE PARK C.1850

LOUISBURGH STREET

TEMPERANCE
HALL

SHORE LANE

MUCKLE PARK

HIGH STREET

TO CAMPS→

This photo of Louisburgh Street, from the east end, shows, on the left the Temperance Hall, a focal point of the town from 1840. It was bought by Mr PercyMcGhan in 1923 and became the Wick Steam Laundry Co. Photo by kind permission of The Wick Society, the Johnston Collection.

Nothing has been discovered during the excavations to indicate the age or who were the occupants of the dwelling now exposed to view. Not a vestige of wood, iron, or even pottery, has yet been come upon. Peat ashes were found on the hearthstone, but no appearance of a "brace" or vent could be traced. Some animal bones, with a few fish bones of a large size, and the under stone of a common old quern, constitute the entire find.

Later the Ensign continued: "Since the foregoing was written, the workmen at the excavations referred to, have come across a number of ancient coins. These were found at the east corner of the old house, among the debris, when removing a huge block of stone at the foundations. The coins discovered, about twenty in number, are much defaced, but can be so far deciphered as to fix their date to that of the reign of the James' a period of two hundred years from 1406, when James First succeeded his father Robert the Third, to 1603, when James the Sixth, on the death of Queen Elizabeth, ascended the English throne. The greater part of these coins are silver groats of the period mentioned, but the metal is of an inferior quality, as may be seen from the large amount of verdigris with which they are encrusted. On one of the pieces the circle lines on both sides are of the rope pattern. The obverse, shows a full face, long and thin, with flowing hair terminating in a deep curl. The crown, which appears to be too large for the head that supports it, has a full fleur-de-lis in the centre, with smaller ones on either side. On the band of the crown is a line of pellets, doubtless indicating the position of the jewels. On the King's left, at the neck, is a small saltire, and two at the termination of a word on the outer legend. This coin on the King's right, is much defaced, and consequently the existence of a fleur-de-lis, or sceptre, cannot be discovered. The legend on the obverse is much too blurred to be rendered legible. The reverse has two circles quartered by the Saint Andrews cross or saltire. The legend on the outer circle is, like that on the obverse, illegible, but on the inner circle the legend, "villa edbvrg" is clearly defined. In each of the two opposite angles of the cross there is a crown, while in the other two angles there are three pellets divided by two annulets. From the description now given, and from the fact that the letter R on the reverse is almost similar to B, numismatists will recognise the coin as a Groat from the reign of James Third. This is the King in whose reign the Earl of Angus received the title of "Bell the Cat," and through whose instrumentality the King's ignoble and overbearing ministers – Cochrane, a builder; Rogers, a musician; Torphichen, a fencing master; Andrews, an astrologer; Hommil, a tailor; and Leonard, a smith, were all hung on Lauder Bridge."

For the two hundred years after 1503 this area was owned by at least five Baillies of Wick and one provost. By the end of the 17th Century the two areas came into the possession of Baillie Robert Calder and his eldest son John (by his first wife Anna Doull). Baillie John Calder was succeeded by his son, William, who was Baillie and Town Clerk of Wick, and his only child, Isabel, became proprietrix of the subjects. Isabel married David Sutherland, merchant, who later became a Baillie, and she disposed of the properties to William Davidson, fish curer of Wick, a nephew of her husband, reserving her own and husband's life rent therein. William Davidson, who died in 1832, was succeeded by his son, William Davidson, surgeon, the last vassal entered to the subjects, which then came into the possession of Provost Rae.

The High Street of the 1840s has been completely rebuilt and keeping our bearings is a little more difficult, as there were no buildings from the foot of Shore Lane to the foot of John Street. The first here on the west side of John Street was the house of William Bain, set back from the road with a low wall enclosing a courtyard. Mr Bain and his sons, Alexander, John, and James, carried on a fish curing business as previously mentioned (see page 51). John became a Fishery Officer. The Bain's curing station was a little upriver from where the Service Bridge stands today.

George Simpson built a property next to the Bain's, not in line with the house, but in line with the front wall of the courtyard. He had windows in the gable, overlooking the courtyard, and with views of the bay. No town planning restrictions in those days.

Next to this were the first offices of The Northern Ensign newspaper. The publishing and editorial office were on the ground floor and the composition room on the first floor which again was reached by a set of external steps. The Ensign was printed on a Columbian press at the rate of one every two minutes, with the strongest apprentice helping Donald MacDonald with the heavy bar. The newspaper's motto was "an injury done to the meanest subject, is an insult upon the whole constitution". Its first leading article was on the subject, "a fair day's pay for a fair day's work, and, a fair day's work for a fair day's pay. The first circulation numbers are unknown, but every newspaper had to carry a red one penny stamp and there was a heavy tax on paper, so there would be a financial risk in printing too many.

A regular visitor to the Ensign office was Mr James Bremner C.E. - almost always on a Friday. He would come in and take his seat on a low set of steps outside the counter and, facing the door, crack jokes, tell anecdotes and relate some of his adventures. Lady Glenorchy, who had a great interest in the schemes of The British Fisheries Society, went on a tour of the various creeks and harbours of the north east coast, all the way round to Cape Wrath, and on to the western isles. For her purpose

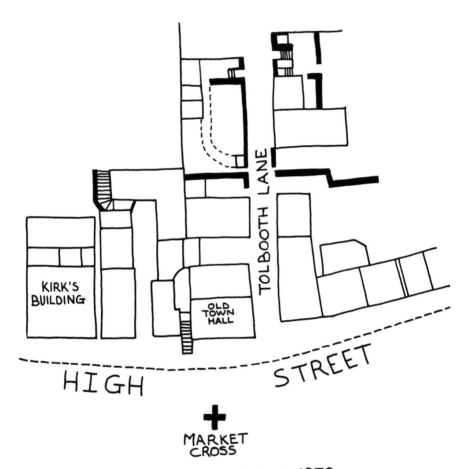

TOLBOOTH LANE

KIRK'S BUILDING

OLD TOWN HALL

HIGH   STREET

✝
MARKET
CROSS

TOLBOOTH LANE AREA   C.1870
ALSO KNOWN AS
TIBETH VENNEL AND POST OFFICE LANE

she had fitted out a herring fishing boat into a not uncomfortable yacht. Mr Bremner accompanied her on the tour of inspection, giving his expert opinion on all the places visited. He had no end of tales of their adventures on the trip. What a pity he never thought, or had the time, to set all his tales down on paper.

Stepping along the street we pass a baker's shop run by John Sutherland, then George Brims boot and shoe shop, arriving at George Auld's, Drug and Fruit Store, a shop with a bulging, bay type window. Apparently Mr Auld always had a cask of "sooples" at the shop door and Wick–ed boys would knock the cask over scattering sooples far and wide. A soople was the business end of a flail, and would be a stout piece of durable wood, not given to splitting easily, about three to four feet long. Mr Auld was a staunch teetotaller, a pillar of the Temperance Society, and was capable of delivering a good speech. A fellow merchant came onto his shop one day and, after being served, made a nasty comment on the large range of goods in which Mr Auld dealt. The comment rather upset Mr Auld and he retorted, " Sir I was in business in this town long before you came, and I will still be in business long after you have been ignominiously kicked out of it." Apparently this almost came to pass. The rooms above Mr Auld's were Mrs Dunnett's coffee rooms and lodgings. The lodgers were mostly the people who came to the town with packs of goods to sell, the aforementioned cheap johns, all sorts of stall holders and on one occasion a German Band! She would be quieter in the winter months but, in the fishing season, it was a case of no room at the Inn.

Next along, we come to Swanson and MacBeath, another boot and shoe shop. The main business of the shop was attended to by David MacBeath. Mr Swanson, his brother-in-law was described as a sort of sleeping partner, but rather wide awake!

We are now on the East corner of Tolbooth Lane, on the site now occupied by Woolworth's, the former North of Scotland Bank building, which opened in 1886.

In the 18th Century, this was the site of the town jail, or Tolbooth.

The premises on the corner was occupied by several people over some years in the middle of the 19th Century. There was a Mr Waters, a draper, Mr Sutherland, a shoe maker, another draper whose name is lost in the mists of time but whose nickname was Manchester; whether this was his place of origin, or whether he favoured that city as his supply source we will never know. Then came Mr James Reiach who was later Provost of our town.

Above Mr Reiach's shop was Mrs Doull's coffee rooms and lodging house, and she was assisted in the business by her two daughters. Mrs Doull's husband William, and her son, had been fishermen and were both lost in the terrible storm of August 19th, 1848 which went down in history as Black Saturday. Mr Doull, managed to get his boat into the harbour mouth but it struck the end of the south quay; the crew managed to scramble up the back of the quay. Mr Doull turned to help his son when a heavy wave swept them both away and they were never seen again. Although thirty seven men lost their lives on that awful day, Mr Doull and his son were the only two from Wick, a further six were from Pulteneytown and one from Staxigoe. All of the others were from Lewis and various parts of Caithness and Sutherland. Mrs Doull's was a very quiet establishment, popular with teetotallers, many of whom were regular patrons, especially on market days. The entrance to the house was round the corner in Tolbooth Lane and opposite was Mrs MacKay's public house, which she ran with her daughter. Mrs MacKay was a widow, but then remarried and became Mrs Bruce. Unfortunately her second husband died, then her daughter married a policeman by the name of Swanson and moved out, and so she was left to cope by herself, which she did rather splendidly. In spite of her occupation, Mrs Bruce was a staunch teetotaller.

Across the lane, and we are on the site which today is occupied by Mackay's Stores.

The first shop was yet another shoemaker, William Mowatt. All of the shoemakers were just that, all made to measure, hand made, and of course, no sewing machines. When Mr Mowatt died the shop was taken by James Sinclair, Watchmaker. Peter Mackenzie was next door, in his draper shop he was not a Wick man, but had married a Wick lady. He usually "imported" his assistants from the country areas and one time employed a lad from Halkirk, who of course lived in. A relative of Mr Mackenzie, who was staying with him at the time, and was fond of a joke, took it into his head to "put one over on the lad." He arranged with the servant girl to put knives and forks on the breakfast table for the porridge and milk and made sure everyone was in on the joke. When all were seated, and the porridge served, our joker picked up his knife and fork and said, "well my lad, I suppose that up your way the spoon is still used for the porridge, you will not be used to the knife and fork?" "oh yes", said the youth picking up his knife and fork, "we've been using knives and forks for the porridge for a long time now." After a good laugh, the spoons were dished out.

Above these shops was the old Town Hall. Outside steps gave access, the steps today would be roughly between MacKays Stores and Lloyds T.S.B. William Brims had it as his showroom, dealing in new and second hand furniture, mostly second hand. He was also an auctioneer, and quite

ANGUS HENDERSON

Angus Henderson, the no nonsense publican.

successful. His foreman was a man by the name of John Budge and two of his apprentices were Henry Hope and John Cameron. Beside the steps was a short lane that ran up towards Louisburgh. At the mouth of this lane was John Phimister's coal yard, and at the end of the lane lived David Davidson, the carter, whose wife kept a cow and sold milk.

Again we turn to Wicker who tells us: "Mrs Davidson was a very nice woman, if, as sometimes happened, our rest peat burnt out before morning, Mrs Davidson was usually able to give us a bit of kindling, and as always, lent us her syer when we had sowans to sye." There's a good piece of old Caithness dialect! Maybe to the present generation, more understandable if it was written, "and, as always, lent us her strainer when we had steeped oats to strain." I prefer the former. Sowans was the sids (husks of oats) and oatmeal, steeped or soaked for up to a week and then strained and the liquid kept. After a day or so, the top liquid was disposed of, or sometimes used in baking, and the lower, thicker layer, the sowans, was used as a drink. This could also be boiled and made into porridge, sometimes referred to as "broon porridge." What a feed, sowans an' broonplate!

Just down the lane from the Davidson's was Angus Henderson's Public House. Angus came from the Freswick area; he was a big man, tall, quite stout and very quietly spoken. His house was the gathering place for all the folk from his home area and he was most particular in the running of his establishment. If any of his customers became quarrelsome or belligerent, they would be quietly admonished and if it came to a threat of fisticuffs he would take one man under each arm and deposit them outside. We turn again to Wicker for his memories of Mrs Henderson:

"Mrs Henderson was a very diligent little woman. I remember one winter morning about 6.30 being sent to the house, where I found Mrs Henderson in the middle of a big baking of oat bannocks, the thin sort, which were usually set out on a tray with a dram. There was a big fire of peat on the hearth in beautiful condition for the baking, and a row of bannocks set all around it, and a lot more finished off on the table. What a comfortable look there was to the whole performance."

On the street in the gable of the house was John Mackenzie's shop; this was the shop that James Donaldson had before he moved to the premises vacated by Waters and Mowat in Bridge Street. John was a brother of Peter Mackenzie and, like his brother, was a draper, but specialized in menswear. The two brothers married two sisters.

Now we are at that part of the High Street from the end of the Lloyds T.S.B. to Mowat Lane that was completely demolished and rebuilt in the early nineteen seventies. Before that time this area was home to what

LONDON WAREHOUSE.

FRESH ARRIVALS.

THE Public are respectfully apprised of a Fresh Arrival of Goods at the LONDON WAREHOUSE, WICK. The Stock consists of a Rich, Rare, and Valuable Assortment of all Descriptions of **British and Foreign Manufactured Goods**, All of which will be disposed of at ASTONISHINGLY LOW PRICES,

The Stock is fresh from the Markets, and in splendid condition; and the quality is such as to keep up the character which the Warehouse has hitherto sustained. Amongst almost innumerable other Articles, is a collection of

Gold and Silver Watches, Guards, and Chains. Ladies' and Gentlemen's Gold Rings, of all sizes.; Gold and Silver Pencil Cases; Gold and Silver Brooches; Scotch Peeble Brooches; Gold Ear-Drops; Ladies' Hair Bracelets, &c., &c. Single and Double-Barrelled Guns, Pistols; Powder Flasks, Percussion Caps. Writing Desks, Work Boxes, Dressing Cases, Tea Caddies, Tea Chests, Knitting and other Boxes. American Clocks, Chinese and French Time-Pieces, Spring Clocks. French, Chinese, and German Accordions, Fiddles, Flutes, and Musical Snuff-Boxes. A Splendid Stock of Oil Paintings, containing Views of Scotland, &c. Tables and Trays, in Papier Mache, very beautiful and costly. Tea-Pots, Tea-Trays, and an immense assortment of China in Sets; Crystal Tumblers, Decanters, Dessert Dishes, Jelly and Pickle Dishes, Cruets, and Stands, Wine and Water Glasses, &c. Cutlery of all Descriptions. A rich and extensive quantity of Bohemian and other Ornaments. Albata Plate. Table Forks and Spoons; Tea Spoons, Dessert Spoons, Toast Racks, Soup Dividers. Bear's Grease, Circassian Cream, Hair Dye, Soaps, of all kinds. Stuffed Birds in Globes; Artificial Flowers in Globes. Alabaster Clocks. A Large Variety of Snuff Boxes, Cigar Cases, Meershum Pipes. Cloth, Hair, Nail, and Tooth Brushes; Side and Dressing Combs. A large Stock of Perfumery. Complete Sets of White and Gold China. Swing and Pier Looking-Glasses. Ledgers and Copy Books. And upwards of Four Hundred different Descriptions of Goods: all of which will be found worthy of public notice, and Extraordinarily cheap.

Important Announcement.

Mr ARNOLD returns his grateful thanks for past favours, and respectfully intimates, that in consequence of the immense size of his Stock, he has been able to purchase it on such terms as will enable him to dispose of it TWENTY-FIVE PER CENT. cheaper than any in the trade. Wick, Dec. 29, 1853.

Charles Arnold's London Warehouse, a real Aladdin's cave of wonders. Where today could you buy a double barrelled gun, a teapot, and a fiddle all from the same shop.

was known as Nicolson's Buildings but, in the mid 19th Century, was Kirk's Buildings, after David Kirk who had the building erected. The first shop in this building was the drapery store of William Kirk (no relation to David). At one point in the life of his business, Mr Kirk was obliged to serve a summons on one of his customers for a debt owed. When the case was over Mr Kirk was asked by a friend who had met him in the street, "Have you gained your case?" "No," replied Mr Kirk, " but I've exposed her!"

After Mr Kirk's day the shop was taken by Mr Richard Wallace, who had come from the south. He had a very miscellaneous stock and also sold sweets of a kind not seen in Wick before, Tom Thumb drops etc., but he did not meet with much success and after a while returned south. Later the shop was taken over by Mr Charles Arnold who stocked a wide variety of goods and traded as "London Warehouse." What a place that must have been; everything from double barrelled guns to alabaster clocks, and from Meerschaum pipes to accordions, a regular bazaar. The other shop was that of David Kirk, who was a very successful Grocer, Baker, and Spirit Merchant. After Mr Kirk's death, his wife and daughter carried on the business for years. Their dwelling house was above the shop and on the floor above was William Georgeson, Tailor, who lived and worked in the premises. On the top floor was William Bain, who was also a tailor. Both of those gentlemen had a signs on the front of the building that could be read from the street. Above the shop that was originally William Kirk, the Misses Waters had their dressmaking business.

Stepping along the street we come to a small shop, set a little back from the road and a step below street level; in modern terms roughly where the Electricity shop is today. It becomes difficult to place these shops exactly as even the census do not name small lanes, describing them as "back of High Street." However we know that the shop belonged to George Bain, a Bower man, who was a meal dealer, and ran the business with his sister and a nephew, Charles Gunn, who lived with them. Our friend and fount of knowledge "Wicker" knew him well and wrote: " Charlie was a studious youth who attended Mackenzie's school and carried off rather more than his share of prizes, and was also pretty successful at taking prizes in competitions. He was little chap, and rather proud of his skills at legerdemain (tricks and magic) Charlie later went to London and lived there a year or two, then he was nominated for surveyor of taxes, and went to Edinburgh to sit the exam. When it was over he told me that he thought it was all right, - it was, his paper on book keeping was perfect, and he got the appointment in Edinburgh a few days later. Unfortunately he did not live very long in his new sphere. "

Next comes an unnamed lane, (by the time of the ordnance survey of 1872, the whole area had changed so it is difficult to place this lane exactly). On the right hand side, the Misses Alexander lived, Christian and Helen, and had their dressmaking business. At the end of the lane and up an outside stair, was the carpentry and joiner shop of James Mackay. He had an excellent business, employed several men, and for a time was the leading business of its kind in the town but, latterly, he did very little. On the opposite side of this wee lane lived a Mr and Mrs Coghill, who had a son Sandy who worked for Pickfords in London. They also had a grandson who was precentor in the United Free Church for a time.

Back on the High Street we arrive in the shoemaker's shop owned by George Manson. He, like others, sold oil for the gooseneb lamps and when Mr Sandison, in Bridge Street died, George got most of his "oily" customers. This shop, like the shops on either side was a step down from the pavement and only had one window beside which Mr Manson worked. This shop became a sort of evening forum, where five or six men would gather to discuss trade, politics, markets etc., George Manson's son carried on the business after his father's death, but by that time paraffin had come in and the debating club was no more. Maybe they joined the Mercantile Debating Society! Mr Manson's neighbour was Mrs McEwen, a grocer and pastry cook. Wicker in his late years remembers her from his boyhood: " she made nice looking and sweet smelling items, shortbread, jam tarts, gingerbread, and all sorts of fine things, can't say how they tasted – never got as far as that, a halfpenny's worth of snaps (6) from Mr Kirk's was the extent of my treat, and that only on high occasions. Mrs McEwen's oven was in the shop, which was very small, and anyone could tell what was cooking as they passed her door. Later she moved to a shop by Killimster toll and died there."

A Difficult Customer

Next in line was Fraser Macbeath, grocer and meal dealer, who was succeeded by William Bain, shoemaker, who by all accounts had a very good business and was a very decent man. His neighbour was James Craig, Tinsmith. Captain Tudor, who was the Harbour Master at this time, had lost the cap of his spy glass and although he had advertised the loss and offered a reward of five shillings (25p) for its return, it was not found, so he called on Mr Craig and ordered a new cap. Mr Craig wanted to make a good job for the Captain, who was a very particular gentleman, and so he got a piece of German silver and made, what he thought, was a very good job. When the Captain called, he examined the cap, asked how much, and paid the half crown (12½p) asked and left the shop without a word. About an hour later he returned and in no pleasant manner asked Mr Craig why he just didn't give the cap back and get the reward, instead of trying to palm it off as his own work and charging half a crown. The Tinsmith was dumbstruck and then showed the irate Captain the piece of silver, and pointed out where he had cut out the rim and end piece. The Captain left, but was not in any way convinced. Three days later he returned again, but this time to beg Mr Craig's pardon for his earlier charge. The original cap had been found by himself in his own house. He then complimented Mr Craig on his fine workmanship and laid the two caps side by side on the counter, they were identical! I suppose that this story shows us two things, 1) the Captain was a gentleman, and 2) the Tinsmith was a craftsman.

Above these two shops lived the Misses Nimmo and John Harrold, who was an army pensioner. Up the lane was the shop of William Waters. I think this lane was the one that led into the area which became Farquhars Court, this would be between the west end of Boot's and Hugo Ross' tackle shop. William Waters was a wood turner and made, among other things, spinning wheels. He worked at them all year round and, by the end of the fishing season, his shop would be overflowing with them but, when the highlanders settled up at seasons end, they virtually emptied his shop.

The next shop was on the corner of Mowatt's Lane. In the middle of the Twentieth Century this was home to the famous Bowles Bakery. In the mid-19th Century it was the shop of William Geddes, a meal dealer. Away back in the 1790s this was the site of what was then the only bakery in Wick, run by a lady whose name is lost in time. She baked twice a week, Wednesday and Saturday, and because of the shortage of cereals such as wheat, anyone wanting a loaf would have to order three days in advance and would be supplied strictly in turn. Lots of people lived up Mowatt's Lane; the 1841 census lists seventy people living there. Whether this was actually in the lane itself or in the vicinity is not clear. At the top of the steps were two single storey thatched cottages; Isabella Young lived in one, and opposite, lived, and worked John Macpherson the Tailor. At the foot of the steps was Miss Geddes' sewing school, and facing the street yet another gable end shop was Sutherland, the Painter, a business which employed several men. Later this became a fancy goods shop run by a Miss Bain. Next up the High Street was a house, again gable to the street, and with a garden in front, considered to be a "swell" house in its day; this belonged to a Mr Sandison, and when he left for the south it was taken by Mr Robertson, Ironmonger.

Just past the Robertson house was a lane, still there today and called Baptist Lane, which leads up to the Nethercliffe Hotel. In the mid-19th century it contained a couple of houses and the Baptist Church, which was erected by Mr Robert Craig, shoemaker, one of the leading members, in conjunction with Mr William Petrie, who advanced some £350 on the building, which, unfortunately did not survive the "great 1970s redevelopment." This church or hall was used, during the week, as a school, run by Mr George Farquhar, who, incidentally, married one of the two Misses Nimmo. In his young days George had been a soldier and was taken prisoner by the French, where he learned the language thoroughly

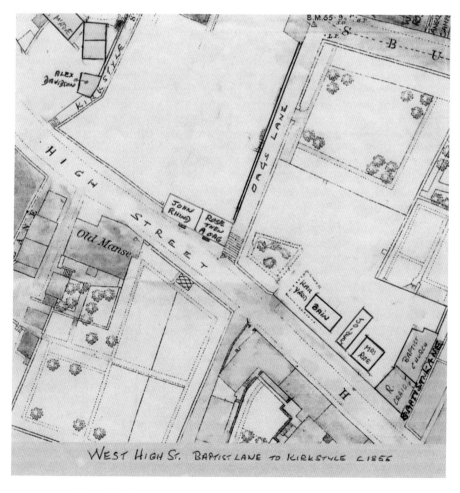

West High Street, Baptist Lane to Kirkstyle c1855.

and so he had many pupils keen to learn. He was well known about the town and used to walk up and down the High Street, always with a quid in his mouth (chewing tobacco) and sometimes a sample of the juice on his lapel. He died in 1862 aged 73, only a year after his wife, who was 80.

The Baptist congregation met in their church on Sundays, with Rev. R.C. Sowerby as minister, and Baillie Waters as his right hand man. Baillie Waters had in fact, single handed, acted as pastor for a number of years before Rev. Sowerby came to Wick in 1848, and continued as co-pastor until his death. In the house below lived Mr John Farquhar, a worthy gentleman, much in demand for concerts and soirees. He was the leader of the "John O' Groat Band," a man with a reputation for efficiency and punctuality. At the top of the steps was a gate which opened into Dr Sinclair's garden and led up to his house that is today The Nethercliffe Hotel, but then was Montpellier House. At the bottom of the lane, facing the High Street, was shoemaker Robert Craig, referred to above, who lived in the house above the shop. After Mr Craig died, his daughter, Teenie, ran a school in the house and taught close on two generations of Wickers. Her principal lesson books were the Bible and the Shorter Catechism. She had the habit of referring to the biblical characters as Mr and Master; thus, it was Mr Moses or Master Samuel. Her other teaching benchmarks were, kindness to animals, consideration for the aged, and the beauty of good manners and politeness, which were duly impressed upon her young charges.

A little up from Mr Craig's (where the Post Office is today) was Mrs Rae's house. She was famous for her shortbread and had the "gentry" as her customers. She baked in the house but never had a display window. Beside her was a joiner shop with a thatched roof; the joiner's name is lost in time. Next was a very old building with a thatched roof, and with a kailyard attached. This was owned and occupied by an old gentleman by the name of Bain, who had been a ship's Captain trading between Wick and Leith. Wicker, in his writings says that he knew him, and tells us that the old sea dog was known by a nick name that had something to do with a Leith eating house's charge for steak, with or without bread, but he fails to tell us what the name was. We can only guess, tuppence ha'penny perhaps? Who knows. He does, however, tell us that Mr Bain had a peculiar habit that possibly had roots in his seafaring life. When he got out of bed, the first thing he did was to throw open his front door facing High Street, still in his nightwear, to have a look at the weather; a strange sight for passers by.

After the Kirk Disruption of 1843, the new Free Kirk folk were looking for a site for their new Kirk and made Mr Bain an offer for his house and ground, but their offer and Mr Bain's expectations were poles apart.

Mr Bain, the old sea dog takes the morning air.

They made three offers, but to no avail, so they settled on the site in Kirk Lane where the Supermarket is today. When Mr Bain did eventually sell his house, it was said that he got less than the Kirk folk had originally offered. A new house was built on the site, for a Mr William Oag though, tragically, his sweetheart died and he never took occupancy. We are now roughly where the Sports Shop is today.

The lane we know today as Oag's Lane was then called Rose's Lane, with a garden where the ruin of Zig Zags nightclub scars the High Street, and the Rose family house on the other side. The Rose family moved south, and Alexander Oag secured the property, so after a time the lane became Oag's Lane. The next house was that of John Rhind, standing where the garden is now, a very old style house with three steps up to the front door. Between here and Kirkstyle Lane was open ground. The Pipe Band hall, formerly the Parish Church Hall was not built until 1909 and the area beyond this was simply referred to as The Kirkstyle. On the left side where the lane narrows, leading up to Louisburgh, were three properties; Alexander Davidson, Fisherman, lived in the corner house, then came a Sinclair Miller, and along from him, towards Kirkhill, was the workshop of Mr McAdie. He was a joiner and specialized in boat fittings, especially oars. Behind his workshop was the house of Mr James Loutitt, rope-maker, and across the road, the Parish School, today the Scout Hall with Mr James McIvor as teacher. A pair of brothers came from Edinburgh and settled in Louisburgh, John and Bob Panton. Bob was a cabinetmaker and John an early photographer, who had a sort of studio in a shed at the Kirkhill. Bob was also a singer and was much in demand for concerts in the Temperance Hall. There were pioneer photographers before them. Before photography came into vogue, portraits were taken by a system known as Daguerreotype, named so after the inventor of the process, a Frenchman called Daguerre, who died in 1851. Not long after that, one of his disciples came to town and tried for business. He did not stay long, demand was low as each image would cost around six shillings, a deal of money in those days. He was followed by a Mr Meston, who also happened to be a barber, and, as far as I am able to ascertain, had a studio over in the Moray Street area, in a shed or old wash house, and for a time did do some business. The work of those early pioneers was to be totally eclipsed in the coming years by the genius of the Johnston family.

This is the area where, in times gone, the residents were treated to the sight of a drunken cow! She resided with the Keith family in the upper half of a house in Kirkstyle, which was reached by a stone stairway without either handrail or banister. On the evening before Fergusmass Market the cow was treated to a good fill of the new draught, and took more than a cow of her age and experience should have. The following morning, it was reported, that like other fools she thought it necessary to keep up the traditions of Fergusmass with a show of friskiness. As Wildans Keith led her down the stairs, she threw her tail and rear legs in the air, much to the astonishment of Wildans, then after gazing calmly at her master, possibly considering her first efforts a great success, she decided that stairs were an unnecessary inconvenience and sprang into the air, not so much jumping over the moon as speeding to earth at great velocity. Such an effort should have been crowned with glory but, as ever, the best laid plans of mice, men, and cows often come to grief, and that was her final Fergusmass flourish.

We have now reached the top of High Street, and across the road is the Muckle Kirk. Before we tackle the south side of the High Street, we'll have another wee diversion as "Wicker" reminisces about his boyhood in this part of our town.

Barking Kettles and the Islands

"Down at the side of the Glebe wall, behind the Kirk, were the barking kettles. When the kettles were in use it was a rare rendezvous for us youngsters. We used to watch the whole performance, boiling the bark, dipping the nets, turning them with a pole, and finally taking them out. When the boiled bark was taken out, there would be lengths of fine pieces, out of which we would make sneerags. This was before "cutch" was known in Wick as a net preservative. There used to be four or five kettles going at the same time. Down from there, in the river were the islands, one large, and one small, on which the ladies bleached their clothes. The islands were reached by stepping stones – big stones laid about a foot apart, the water was not deep. On the Muckle island, the one highest upriver, there was a pool where Branstickles could be caught, also small eels, white and brown. People who had a big washing of blankets etc., used to light a fire near the quarry and do the tramping in the open air. Sometimes a cow or two got on to the islands, not a pleasing sight to those who had their clothes laid out to bleach, great objection and strong language were made use of on these occasions.

(A Sneerag was a child's toy formed from a pig's foot bone and worked with worsted thread to produce a snoring sound.)

We also played cricket, or rather played at cricket. Mr Mackie was the man who made a start, and got together enough to make a game on a Saturday afternoon or on an evening during the week. George Bain, Peter Grant, Ramage, William Miller jun., two or three of Rev. Lillie's sons from the manse, James Bremner the poet, and others. We didn't always muster a full field, but generally had more than eleven, so we

91

managed to have a game that pleased us. We did not form a club or pay subscriptions, but we did have one bat, a professionally made one. The others I think, as well as the stumps, were home made. The first place that I saw professional cricket being played, was at the Oval, it was an eye-opener to me. Some of the best players were there, Lilywhite, Carpenter, Coffyn, Griffiths, and Lockyer, said to be the best wicket keeper in England. For all that, we thoroughly enjoyed our cricket on the glebe."

Dirty Weekers?

The idyllic scene painted by Wicker is totally at odds with the Wick described by a writer to the Northern Ensign in September of 1853 who signed him or herself simply Elutor. The lengthy letter first tackles the spectre of cholera in the town and goes on. " Why, sir, you well know that the river is universally used for washing when rain water is scarce, and you know that the river islands are used as bleaching greens when garden accommodation is wanting, and you and everybody else knows that the river is kept in a state of beastly and abominable pollution by the presence of huge carcasses lying therein. Just above the bleaching spots, and the shores from which washing water is taken, there are dead horses, cows, dogs and cats, lying all year round. Impregnating the river water with their poisonous emanations until the water can be nothing else but elaborately prepared death." The writer goes on to complain about carcasses lying on the north shore as far out as Proudfoot, as well as on the south shore, while the east point of the harbour, "at low tide, is so volatile and corrupt that the very existence of people in Lower Pulteney is to be wondered at." The letter finishes, " north, south, east, or west, the state of matters is all the same, filth, corruption, and death."

The People go Out

Before we leave the Muckle Kirk, we should take note that these had been troubled times. The Rev. Charles Thompson had been admitted to this charge on the 17th September 1840. He was of the Evangelical Party of the Church and arrived in turbulent times in the national Church, which ended in the Disruption of 1843. I do not wish to dwell on the details and causes of that disruption but, in its simplest form, the Heritors of the Kirk, the landed gentry, had the say on who should or should not be the minister and could actually pick a minister without reference to the people and install him into the charge. The people regarded this as intrusion and rebelled saying, no more; we will choose our own ministers, we want out of the established Kirk, we want a Free

The Rev. Charles Thompson.

The Rev. William Lillie MA., DD.

Kirk. The culmination of this was a huge meeting, or Convocation, held in Edinburgh in November of 1842, where all in favour of "going out" would sign the resolution, and then return to their Kirks and lead their people out. In the case of Wick it was a wee bit different. The Rev Thomas Brown D.D. in his book, Annals of the Disruption, which was published in 1890, writes:

"There were cases indeed, in which the people went beyond their ministers in their zeal for the cause. Mr Thompson of Wick, belonged to the evangelical party of the church, but, as the crisis approached, he felt considerable perplexity, and, on returning from the Convocation, he gathered his people together on the 28th November in order to explain, which he did at some length, the reasons why he had NOT seen it his duty to sign the resolutions. (to leave the established Church) During his address the congregation sat looking at each other, much astonished, and after the meeting had been dismissed, the people, on the motion of Mr Davidson, Banker, sat still, elected a chairman, and asked Mr Thompson to listen to the proceedings. They went on to express their views, with much personal respect to their pastor, but in direct opposition to the sentiments of his address. It was then proposed that solemn thanks should be offered up to God, for the grace which had been vouchsafed to the 350 members of the convocation who had bound themselves to "go out" and this was done in a most impressive manner by Mr Donald George. At a second meeting held shortly after, they formally adopted the Convocation resolutions, and the result was that Mr Thompson saw it to be his duty to go along with his people a resolution that was received with much satisfaction," So it was, that in the case of Wick Parish Church, it was the people, who led the minister out.

Although we make much mention of The Parish Church, The Free Church and The Baptist Church, there were other persuasions alive and very well in our town in the mid 19th. Century. Certainly the Roman Catholics had formed a congregation by 1832, and by 1836 had built their Chapel. There were also Wesleyans, Methodists, Congregationalists, Evangelists and Seceders, enough to satisfy most religious needs of the day. It is good to note the tolerance and acceptance of the rights and beliefs of others. Fortunately this kind of tolerance is still with us today.

Back to the High Street

The next lane down from the Kirk is St. Fergus Lane, which of course led down to St. Fergus Well (in older days the Kirk was known as St. Fergus

Kirk). This is a steep lane and would be quite a climb for anyone carrying a couple of kits of water.

Now we come to a very old building which was originally the Kirk manse, but was at this time lived in by Mrs Barbara Macleay and the Misses Macleay, family of the now deceased Mr William Macleay who had been Provost of Wick from 1814 – 1818. Mr Macleay was the first master of Lodge St Fergus 252 (later 466) and held that office from its consecration in December of 1795 until 1805, although the Lodge went into abeyance from 1799 – 1802, due to the large number of members who were serving King and Country. Incidentally, one of the Macleay girls married the Rev Robert Phinn, minister of the Parish Church from 1813 to 1840. Their son, Rev. Dr. Kenneth Macleay Phinn, became a well-known preacher and prominent Kirk man of his day. He was named Kenneth in honour of his mothers uncle, Kenneth Macleay Esq. of Keiss, who in 1818 had commissioned Mr James Bremner to build the harbour at Keiss.

In the mid 20th century it was known as Dr Leask's house.

After their time, the house was acquired by Mr James Sinclair, meal dealer. There was always a fine garden in front of this house and, back in the mid-19th Century there was a nice green, at riverside level, where the Highlanders gathered on Sundays during the fishing season.

Macleay Lane runs down the east side of the garden wall and, this was where Mr William Miller, Church Officer, lived. At the top east side of this lane was the Aberdeen Bank, and the house of Mr Adam, the manager, was on the bank on the High Street above Graham Begg's Electrical store. Mr Adam's father lived with him, an excellent gardener, who kept a fine garden to the rear of the house. Mr Adam's son, Thomas, and a Mr Fielding were clerks in the bank. Mr Adam also had a flag yard in Lower Pulteney where the stone was sawn for paving etc. This project was run by his son, James. This part of High Street was a row of terraced houses that ran down to Houston's Restaurant. At the end, next to where Houston's is today, was a house which stood back from the street with a small paved courtyard in front. Charles Arnold had it for his business,

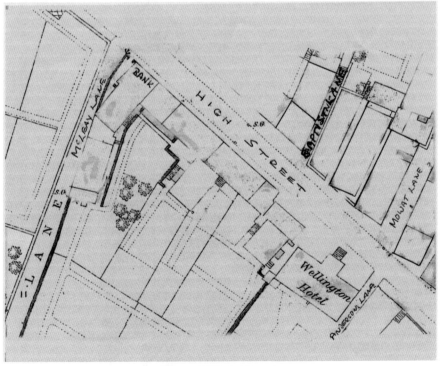

Map of High Street.

97

How Alex Corner's property and John Kirk's hoosie may have looked, with the "blethering wall" between. Today this is the site of The 99p Store and Harrold's Butchers.

but outgrew it and moved to the site already mentioned. It then became a saddlers business run by James Levack, or Leavoch.

The Wellington Hotel (now Houston's) came next, run by Mr and Mrs John Levack. The Wellington was also a posting establishment, with the stables down in Andersons Lane. At the top of and on the east side of Andersons Lane that is next to the Wellington, was the drapery shop of Mr Alexander Corner; here again we have a property built on a steep hill, with gable end to the street, and so built that the shop area was on the first floor, but on street level, and on the east side a stone stair led down to the house on the lower level. On street level a low stone wall with a flat top ran along to the next shop and house of John Kirk. This wall, according to our friend Wicker, was a favourite resting place in the warm weather, especially in the long summer evenings, and was much appreciated by the inhabitants of the close across the street. All the news of the Parish could be gleaned here, and all topics were keenly discussed, but usually in a friendly and genial manner. Over the wall the ground dropped down ten to twelve feet and overlooked a courtyard in front of Mrs Corner's house.

Now we are on the corner where Harrold's butchers stands today at the top of Kirk Lane. This was the site of what was called "John Kirk's Hoosie"and was built along the lines of Mr Corner's, gable to the street, but, because the slope was less here, the first floor was some feet above street level. Mr Kirk overcame this by building a platform at first floor level, accessed by a flight of steps at either side. The platform continued around the side of the house, consequently, there was no pavement in front. Town planning? Everyone built to please themselves! Mr Kirk's shop extended the full length of the first floor. It was in the loft of this building that the local Baptist Church folk first met, until the church was built in Baptist Lane in the early 1820s. Their baptisms in those days were carried out in the river at the Cruives, up past where the railway tunnel is today.

Wicker describes Mr Kirk's shop for us:

"It was a drapery and grocery business; drapery in all its branches, Mr Kirk kept all that was needed to clothe man or woman. The front shop was a nice big room, with a counter, from behind which, Mr Kirk welcomed his clients. Behind this there were two or three rooms, where customers who were not too anxious that the whole town would know what they bought, were taken, quietly seated, and had an assistant told off to attend, and to wait upon them, a most excellent arrangement."

Well, well; modern department stores take note, personal shopping was alive and well in Wick all those years ago. The dwelling house was at the end and below the shop down in Kirk Lane. The assistants mostly lived on the premises; staff names we know were George Bell, John Horne, James Henderson, Robbie Gunn, Danny Bain and James Manson. When Mr Kirk died in 1863 aged 77years, John Horne took over the business.

Quite substantial money

Mr Kirk had been very successful in his business life and left a number of bequests. J.T.Calder, in his Civil and Traditional History of Caithness, details them thus; Mr John Kirk, merchant, Wick who died in March 1863, provided that £10 per annum shall be divided among the various schemes of the Free Church, £2.10/- to the Free Church teacher of Wick and a small donation to the Royal Infirmary, Edinburgh. He also provided that on the Friday before New Years Day, the Free Church minister of Wick shall give away to eighty deserving individuals, as many half-crowns; and the Free Church minister of Bower, twenty half-crowns among as many of like character, the same to be known as "John Kirk's New Year's Gift." The interest of a sum of about £9000 was to be applied as follows:- One half for the benefit of decayed labourers and aged females, who had seen better days and are not in receipt of parochial relief; the other half to be devoted to educational purposes in Wick and Bower and to the parish of Canisbay also, should the amount exceed a stipulated sum. The trustees are the Sheriff Substitute of Caithness, the Provost and Baillies of Wick, etc.

The entry to Kirk Lane is more or less the same today as it was all those years ago, with a set of stone steps on either side of the roadway. Across the road, where Cameo Jewellers stands today, was the shop of Baillie Campbell, grocer and spirit merchant; he was a snappy dresser, usually decked out in a frilled shirt with gold pins. This corner was known as Campbell's corner. John Stewart, accountant, had his office next door, with his house above. John Sutherland, shoemaker, was in the last shop in the row. He was a very hard working and active man, and generally had a couple of men working for him. For years he closed his shop on Saturday afternoons, and in the summer he went for a swim every day, at noon, at the North Head. Mr Sutherland was also a fine skater and was usually about the first on the ice when the river froze over; he also took trips to the south and once journeyed to Canada; his experiences over there appeared in the columns of the "Northern Ensign."

The Local Swimmers

A swimming club existed in Wick at this time. There were, as previously mentioned, seven harbours along the north shore; the last two were Black Rock, now the North Baths, and the last harbour, latterly owned by Alexander Wares. Just beyond this, there are two sets of rock

The area of the "Sisters" and the "Kists".

formations, known locally as the "Kists" and " The Sisters", and it was in front of these that the club met. Wicker was evidently a member and tells us that the group called themselves the "Socuir Club" and writes, "fine diving the members displayed, at least we had that idea of it. John Sutherland, shoemaker; James Reiach, draper; James Henderson, book keeper; John Kirk, and others. Charlie Gunn was the secretary. Every day at noon we used to bathe and practice swimming and diving. John Sutherland was the champion swimmer and diver. I've seen him pick up three or four shirt buttons off the ground at a depth of twelve or fourteen feet, with the buttons as far apart as space would permit. He used to bathe in the sea every Saturday, all year round and on every New Year's Day."

I think that the sea bed in this area has changed quite dramatically. Certainly in the author's youth, in the early to mid 1950s, Wares' Harbour had a quite smooth bed of shingle, whereas today it is a jumble of rocks.

We have now come full circle and once again we are standing at Francie Quoys corner.

I hope you have enjoyed this wee dip into a Wick, long, long gone.

The two decades in which all these people lived and worked were undoubtedly exciting and tumultuous times, with the rapid expansion of the town as a major fishing port, the food riots of 1847, the tragedy of Black Saturday in 1848, the War of the Orange in 1859 and the beginning of Stevenson's breakwater in 1863. All this long before the telegraph, real piped water, the harbour extension and the coming of the railway. These are the times we look back on and think, " Ah, the good old days" but were they? My maternal granny, Bella Rosie, spoke freely of the old days. But, if I ever said "good old days" she was always quick to say, "Harry, there was no such thing as good old days, we were only happy because we were ignorant, dinna ye hark back, we've never been as weel off as we are now." I think she got it right.